NEW DIRECTIONS FOR ADULT AND CONTINUING EDUCATION

Susan Imel, *Ohio State University*
EDITOR-IN-CHIEF

Addressing the Spiritual Dimensions of Adult Learning: What Educators Can Do

Leona M. English
Saint Francis Xavier University

Marie A. Gillen
Saint Francis Xavier University

EDITORS

Number 85, Spring 2000

JOSSEY-BASS PUBLISHERS
San Francisco

ADDRESSING THE SPIRITUAL DIMENSIONS OF ADULT LEARNING: WHAT
EDUCATORS CAN DO
Leona M. English, Marie A. Gillen (eds.)
New Directions for Adult and Continuing Education, no. 85
Susan Imel, Editor-in-Chief

Microfilm copies of issues and articles are available in 16mm and 35mm,
as well as microfiche in 105mm, through University Microfilms Inc., 300
North Zeeb Road, Ann Arbor, Michigan 48106-1346.

ISSN 1052-2891   ISBN 0-7879-5364-4

NEW DIRECTIONS FOR ADULT AND CONTINUING EDUCATION is part of The
Jossey-Bass Higher and Adult Education Series and is published quarterly
by Jossey-Bass Inc., Publishers, 350 Sansome Street, San Francisco, California 94104-1342. Periodicals postage paid at San Francisco, California,
and at additional mailing offices. Postmaster: Send address changes to
New Directions for Adult and Continuing Education, Jossey-Bass Inc.,
Publishers, 350 Sansome Street, San Francisco, California 94104-1342.

SUBSCRIPTIONS cost $58.00 for individuals and $104.00 for institutions,
agencies, and libraries.

EDITORIAL CORRESPONDENCE should be sent to the Editor-in-Chief,
Susan Imel, ERIC/ACVE, 1900 Kenny Road, Columbus, Ohio
43210-1090. E-mail: imel.1@osu.edu.

Cover photograph by Wernher Krutein/PHOTOVAULT © 1990.

Jossey-Bass Web address: http://www.josseybass.com

Printed in the United States of America on acid-free recycled paper con-
taining 100 percent recovered waste paper, of which at least 20 percent is
postconsumer waste.

CONTENTS

EDITORS' NOTES

Spirituality! Like dandelions in the spring, the term is cropping up everywhere. There are books, magazine articles, newsletters, conferences, tapes, even Web sites dealing with the subject. The explosion of interest in spirituality gives rise to tantalizing questions: Why this interest now? Is it a response to the spiritual malaise at the end of a thousand-year epoch? Is it merely what is referred to as millennium hype, or disillusionment with materialistic gains? We suspect that Harris's (1996) insight is correct. She says that the hunger for spiritual riches is a "desire for depth in our personal lives on one hand and awareness of realms greater than ourselves on the other" (p. 15). Whatever the reason, interest in spirituality seems to be everywhere, even in such unlikely locations as the corporate boardroom. Posner (1999) tells us, "The workplace spirituality movement is gaining momentum and beginning to penetrate the consciences of the world's corporations. Its most ardent disciples insist it's just in its infancy" (p. 72). A case can be made that we are living in times whose materialistic context confounds individuals who seek a vision of a full life to which they can be faithful. Consequently, interest in spirituality is rapidly gaining momentum.

What is spirituality? Can it be defined? In some respects, it has such a variety of meanings that defining it is like trying to pin jelly to a wall; it does not stick. Miller (1985) refers to it as a "weasel word" (p. 66) and in his view the word is almost meaningless. But there are others who have tried to come to grips with the term. Harris (1996) refers to it as "our way of being in the world in the light of the Mystery at the core of the universe; a mystery that some of us call God" (p. 15). She distinguishes two different and almost opposite meanings of the term *spirituality*—one marked by withdrawal from the world and the other marked by immersion in the world. The latter distinction, which is characterized by a social and political dimension, is what interests us as adult educators. Further clarification from Van Ness (1996) is also helpful. He distinguishes between religious spirituality and secular spirituality. The fact that people are religious does not mean that they are spiritual. As Van Ness points out, "A secular spirituality is neither validated nor invalidated by religious varieties of spirituality. Its status is related to them but separable" (p. 1). In other words, religion is based on an organized set of principles shared by a group, whereas spirituality is the expression of an individual's quest for meaning. Although religion and spirituality may be connected, they are not necessarily.

So, how is spirituality conceptualized in this book? We, the editors, define it as awareness of something greater than ourselves, a sense that we are connected to all human beings and to all of creation. Simply put, authentic spirituality moves one outward to others as an expression of one's spiritual experiences. We concur with Berry (1988) that "spiritual issues are those dealt with in the . . . world of active human existence" (p. 111). Therefore, this book is located in what Berry refers to as "public spirituality" (p. 110) or in what Van Ness (1996) refers to as "secular spirituality" (p. 1).

Given the current interest in spirituality, adult educators today must ask themselves whether they should be concerned about the quest for meaning, or what some writers refer to as the spiritual dimensions of adult education. As editors, our response is a resounding *yes!* This affirmation begs two further questions: Why? and How? In the chapters that follow, the authors provide answers to both questions. They respond in greater detail to the how question, so we elaborate on the why question before we introduce the rest of the volume.

In brief, a great spiritual hunger or search for meaning is under way in the world today (Merriam and Heuer, 1996). Adult educators have paid a great deal of attention to the aesthetic, social, emotional, physical, intellectual, and other aspects of education but have neglected the equally important spiritual dimension. We argue that to omit the spiritual dimension is to ignore the importance of a holistic approach to adult learning as well as the complexity of the adult learner.

The search for a vision of life that transcends contemporary social conventions—the spiritual quest—is not unique to the current times. Pioneers in the field of adult education, such as Basil Yeaxlee (1925) and Moses Coady (1939), consciously or not, drew on thousand of years of spiritual thought in formulating their operational principles and sets of assumptions. They realized that all citizens, of whatever country, should have the opportunity to develop socially, morally, and spiritually, and to benefit economically. Their ideas not only were the product of their generation but also grew from the past. The ideas of justice, service, caring, cooperation, and the dignity of the person are the bedrock on which the field of adult education is built (Gillen, 1998). Coady believed that any adult education endeavor should meet the spiritual as well as the material needs of persons. He believed that these needs should not be compartmentalized but rather integrated into the whole of life. Chapters Three and Seven both refer to Coady's work in order to make their respective cases for the recovery of the spiritual dimension of adult education.

The chapters in this volume will give you, the reader, an inkling of the kind of comprehensive adult education that is happening today through efforts that deliberately address the spiritual dimensions of adult education. We invite you to examine your own practice in light of these chapters and to ask yourself the following questions: What meaning does the spiritual have for me? How do I make sense of or establish meaning in my personal and professional life? Am I addressing the spiritual needs of adult learners? If yes, what are the spiritual characteristics of my practice? If no, would the inclusion of a spiritual dimension in my practice make it more relevant to what is going on in society today? It is our hope that the following chapters, written by adult educators who have incorporated a spiritual dimension into their practice, will stimulate you to reflect on your practice and provide answers to these questions.

Jane Vella and Linda J. Vogel set the stage. In Chapter One, Vella offers a revolutionary new approach to adult learning that she refers to as a "spirited epistemology." Her focus is on adult learners as subjects of or decision makers in their own learning. She points out that such reverence for the learner requires a moral stance for the teacher and the curriculum designer. She explains the several assumptions on which her chapter is based, elaborates on principles and practices for adult educators that will help to make them more accountable to the learner, and speculates on the future use of a spirited epistemology. To make her points, Vella uses stories drawn from her rich personal experiences as a global adult educator.

Vogel's ideas, in the second chapter, expand on the ideas presented in the first chapter. Her focus is on adult educators, specifically on their spiritual lives. As she sees it, teaching and learning that are holistic must be open to and reckon with the spiritual lives of both adult educators and learners. Toward this end, an approach that honors the experience of each person and leaves room for mystery can lead to transformative teaching and learning that engage the transcendent in ways that grow out of different faith traditions. Vogel presents such ideas as exploring our inner lives for insights that inform our questions and answers; tapping our spiritual lives in ways that are life giving, open to difference, and accepting of others; and recognizing that our spiritual lives are nurtured through story, tradition, ritual, hope, creativity, and imagination.

These two chapters provide an excellent introduction to the next two chapters, in which Leona M. English and R.E.Y. Wickett focus on a particular learning process that includes strategies for fostering spiritual development. In Chapter Three, English focuses on informal learning and on three specific strategies: mentoring, self-directed learning, and dialogue. She argues that these strategies are untapped resources that can be used to promote the spiritual development of adult educators and learners, and that they have the potential to help both adult educators and adult learners learn about their ways of relating and being in the world—what this volume refers to as the spiritual dimension of learning.

In contrast to English's stress on informal learning, Wickett focuses in Chapter Four on formal learning. He presents the learning covenant as a way of formalizing the learning relationship as a learning partnership. The covenant, unlike the contract, signals the uniqueness of the teaching bond, the sanctity of the relationship, and the reciprocity among the learner, the adult educator, and the institution. The covenant serves as a spiritual basis of the learning agreement and as a reminder of the importance and sanctity of learning and knowing.

The next four chapters present examples of how a spirited epistemology has been applied in a variety of adult education contexts. Each author draws on her or his experiences and area of expertise. We chose these examples not because they are exhaustive but because they highlight adult education practices that have successfully integrated the spiritual in a manner that is consistent with our definition. In other words, these examples are only the tip of the iceberg. We believe that adult educators in a variety of settings can learn from them.

The subject of Chapter Five, by Lynda W. Miller, is continuing professional education. She points out that nursing education today is moving toward a more holistic approach in which all the dimensions of learning, including the spiritual, are included. She presents a conceptual model for a new initiative in continuing nursing education called parish nursing and describes a parish nursing course she developed based on this model. She explains how the course is constructed and delivered, and presents some feedback from nurses who have taken the course. She challenges other professions to include the spiritual dimension of learning in their continuing education programs.

In Chapter Six, Jeffrey A. Orr presents spiritual practices drawn from his work with Native students. A non-Native, his approach in this chapter is to give voice to Native peoples. Like Vella, he skillfully uses stories as a vehicle for describing how Native people draw spiritual strength from a variety of resources and supports, especially the medicine wheel. The message of the chapter is that the art of communion with the earth, which is so basic to Native ways of knowing, is also basic to all spiritual development. Orr concludes by noting that survival in the future depends more on non-Natives learning from Native peoples than on Native people learning from others.

Wilf E. Bean, in Chapter Seven, draws us into both international and domestic community development. He points out how the spiritual ideals of justice, service, caring, cooperation, and the dignity of the human person are the bedrock on which community development is built. Drawing on his many years of experience working at the international level, Bean emphasizes the importance of both the material and spiritual dimensions of the community development projects carried out in a number of countries. He stresses the organic connection of these two dimensions, and cautions that the neglect of one dimension affects and is affected by the other.

In Chapter Eight, Catherine P. Zeph presents lay formation ministry as a new initiative in adult religious education. In her view, lay ministry education has definite challenges, not the least of which is the inclusion of a strong spiritual component in an intellectually challenging educational program. Her chapter describes in detail the lay formation program in which she works, and highlights the challenges and solutions of putting together such an offering.

It is fitting that we, this volume's editors, should write the last chapter, which gives us the opportunity to highlight concerns and future directions with respect to the spiritual dimension of adult education in light of what has been presented in the preceding chapters. We point out some of the forces that make it difficult to integrate a spiritual dimension into adult education programs, such as lack of understanding about the true meaning of spirituality and lack of practice-based knowledge, as well as forces, both organizational and institutional, that block such initiatives or co-opt them to serve their own selfish ends. We conclude that a more holistic approach to learning, which includes a spiritual dimension, is what is needed in the field of adult education in the years ahead. We also include annotations of books that readers will find interesting and informative.

This issue of *New Directions for Adult and Continuing Education* is truly a collective effort, and we are indebted to everyone who helped us come to grips with the meaning and impact of spirituality today, especially the spiritual dimension of adult education. We also would like to acknowledge the support of the Father Gatto Fund at Saint Francis Xavier in completing this work.

Although we continue to struggle with questions and to challenge each other as we search for answers, we recognize that spirituality is at a new threshold. Referring to this time in history, Ó Murchú (1998) notes that "a new day is dawning over the spiritual landscape and new possibilities for spiritual pilgrimage open up on all sides" (p. 20). These are exciting times—the beginning of a new millennium. We welcome you to these pages and hope that you find the ideas contained between the covers of this volume stimulating and engaging.

References

Berry, T. *The Dream of the Earth*. San Francisco: Sierra Club Books, 1988.
Coady, M. M. *Masters of Their Own Destiny*. New York: HarperCollins, 1939.
Gillen, M. A. "Spiritual Lessons from the Antigonish Movement." In S. Scott, B. Spencer, and A. Thomas (eds.), *Learning for Life: Canadian Readings in Adult Education*. Toronto: Thompson, 1998.
Harris, M. *Proclaim Jubilee! A Spirituality for the Twenty-First Century*. Louisville, Ky.: Westminster/John Knox Press, 1996.
Merriam, S. B., and Heuer, B. "Meaning-Making, Adult Learning and Development: A Model with Implications for Practice." *International Journal of Lifelong Education*, 1996, 15 (4), 243–255.
Miller, R. C. "Process Spirituality and the Religious Educator." In J. M. Lee (Ed.), *The Spirituality of the Religious Educator*. Birmingham, Ala.: Religious Education Press, 1985.
Ó Murchú, D. *Reclaiming Spirituality*. New York: Crossroad, 1998.
Posner, M. "Spirituality Inc." *Enroute*, April 1999, pp. 70–77.
Van Ness, P. H. (ed.). *Spirituality and the Secular Quest*. Vol. 22: *World Spirituality: An Encyclopedic History of the Religious Quest*. New York: Crossroad, 1996.
Yeaxlee, B. A. *Spiritual Values in Adult Education*. 2 vols. London: Oxford University Press, 1925.

LEONA M. ENGLISH *is assistant professor of adult education at Saint Francis Xavier University, Antigonish, Nova Scotia.*

MARIE A. GILLEN *is professor of adult education at Saint Francis Xavier University, Antigonish, Nova Scotia.*

1

This chapter offers a revolutionary new approach to adult learning that involves a radical new concept of education as creative, critical action and of the teacher as resource person, not professor. Through stories of real-life educational encounters, the principles and practices for such an approach are presented.

A Spirited Epistemology: Honoring the Adult Learner as Subject

Jane Vella

The spiritual dimensions of adult education are the human dimensions, and attention to these dimensions makes for excellent, effective adult learning. Recognizing adult learners as the Subjects (capitalized, as Carl Jung taught, in order to emphasize the primacy of the learner) of or decision makers in their own learning involves a moral stance for the teacher, for the curriculum designer, and for the learners themselves. This is a revolutionary new way of looking at learning.

Epistemology is the study of knowing and the art of learning. I urge teachers to work toward a learning-centered approach to their teaching via a *spirited epistemology,* remembering, as St. Augustine said in the fourth century: "No man teaches another anything. All we can do is to prepare the way for the work of the Holy Spirit." The epistemology of which I speak applies to all persons, regardless of whether they are Buddhist, Muslim, Christian, or Sikh, or nurture their spirituality outside of traditional religious frameworks. It is an epistemology grounded in humanity.

I learned this important theory of the learner as Subject not from any philosopher or theorist but from a poignant story told by my Tanzanian friend Anna, a peasant farmer who decided to become a Christian. Anna loved Thomas, who had been baptized after studying the faith with a Roman Catholic priest in a year-long course. Anna was determined to become a Christian. At the end of the course, Anna was told by the very uptight, superconscientious priest (who had apparently never read Augustine!) that she had failed! He told her that she was not ready for baptism. Anna's disappointment was great and, as she told me in Swahili, she dreaded the thought of another year of those dull question-and-answer recitation sessions. "Imenichokoza!" (It tired me out each time!) she said. However, Anna loved Thomas and wanted to marry him as a Christian. She soon realized something that gave her the courage to begin the course for a second year. She said, "Yeye ni binadamu, na mimi ni binadamu pia." (I thought to myself about that priest: he is a human being, and I am a human being, too.) She was prepared to face off with a pompous teacher for another year if that was what it would take to win her love. Anna succeeded, and was baptized and married on the same happy weekend.

Anna taught me that people are the Subjects, or decision makers, not only of their own learning but also in their lives.

The revolutionary assumption that the teacher is accountable to the learner is the linchpin principle on which all the other principles and practices of effective adult education rest. This chapter describes how we, as adult educators, can celebrate with men and women the fact that they are indeed Subjects of their learning and of their lives. When you finish reading the chapter, you will have heard and examined three assumptions about adult learning; defined and described what it means to be a Subject, or decision maker, in your own learning; heard a number of stories demonstrating the validity of the assumptions and the practicality of this approach; defined a spirited epistemology; reviewed six principles and practices that guide adult educators in the use of such an approach; defined an axiom and read some axioms for effective adult education; and previewed the next chapter. This is my covenant with you, Subject to Subject.

Assumptions

1. Human beings are designed to be Subjects, or decision makers, in their own lives and learning.
2. Each learning event is a moment of spiritual development in which people practice being what they are—Subjects of their own lives and learning.
3. Transformation is not grasping an external set of information, knowledge, or skills, but rather a change into one's new self, informed by the new knowledge and skills.

These assumptions are the basis of an approach to adult education that respects the learner as Subject of the learning. *Respect* comes from the Latin words *re*, "again," and *spectare*, "to look at." Look at the learner again! What a simple task for the educator. Such an attitude is more caught than taught. Jesus showed that he knew this when in response to the first curious disciples, who asked, "Where do you live?" he replied, "Come and see." All great spiritual teachers invite us to have a conscious respect for ourselves, our neighbors, and our world.

As I examine each separate assumption, I build a framework for particular practices that are congruent with these assumptions.

ASSUMPTION 1. *Human beings are designed to be Subjects, or decision makers, in their own lives and learning.*

Darryl Burrow, a bright young man from New Orleans, is director of the Annie E. Casey Foundation Jobs Initiative in New Orleans. This program educates the hard-to-employ so that they are able to get good jobs and work with resources in the community to develop work opportunities. Darryl invited Global Learning Partners, Inc., to share their revolutionary approach to adult education both with the community organizers who recruit for the program and teach adults participating in the program, and with the faculty of the community college, who are resources to the program.

Global Learning Partners insists on the importance of the site of any learning event, what we call the *Where* of the Seven Steps of Planning: *Who, Why, When, Where, What for, What,* and *How.* As Subject of his own learning, Darryl used his knowledge of this requirement to arrange creatively the sites for the two courses. The community college professors would take the course in the downtown community center, and the community organizers would take it at the community college learning center. Such creativity and respect for context is what we celebrate and what we invite when we believe that the learner is Subject of what he or she does with what is learned.

Being Subject of one's own learning also means that one reconstructs a theory or skill to fit one's own context. This is what philosophers do when they take the work of previous philosophers and prepare their own philosophy. Each artist composes standing on the shoulders of his or her teachers. When a spirited epistemology is used, learners are invited to "compose" what they are learning so that it fits their life and context.

Paulo Freire (1970) describes the *banking* system of education, whereby the teacher deposits information and gets back from learners that same information on tests. This is the farthest thing from what we do when we use a spirited epistemology. Being Subject of one's own learning means hard work, severe discipline, and intense effort. Being Subject does not mean taking a subjective view of what is being learned, but learning new theories and skills to the utmost and then making sure that what has been learned fits one's context. This is what Darryl did with the Seven Steps of Planning in his creative use of the Where. Those who took part in the program celebrate that in New Orleans they learned the theory well and were creative and faithful enough to make that theory work in the New Orleans context.

ASSUMPTION 2. *Each learning event is a moment of spiritual development in which people practice being what they are—Subjects of their own lives and learning.*

Learning tasks, not teaching tasks, are the heart of an accountable design in a spirited epistemology. The design of a learning event, a class or meeting, or a training session can afford opportunity for engaged learners to be involved in active re-creation of the skill or theory or attitude being studied as Subjects. Learning tasks, not teaching tasks, are the heart of an accountable design in a spirited epistemology.

For the Governor's Conference on Learning in Vermont in May 1998, I had the pleasure of designing, as the keynote address, a one-hour session in which 150 educators worked assiduously on Johnson and Johnson's (1987) adaptation of Kurt Lewin's (1951) twelve principles of learning. The educators worked in pairs. They read Lewin's principles, which were on placards on the wall, and selected the ones that spoke most directly to their experience as educators. The ensuing dialogue was profound and enlightening. Men and women who had worked with one another for years discovered unique perspectives, unexpected insights, and wisdom. Their learning was in the doing and the deciding. It was a well-spent hour.

I hope that today they remember that keynote address as a moment in their development as individuals and as people working together to improve education. Every such moment is a spiritual moment simply because we are human, that is, spiritual beings. The practice of being and acting as Subjects enabled the participants to share more than the information about Lewin's theories of learning that was on the placards. They also shared themselves.

ASSUMPTION 3. *Transformation is not grasping an external set of information, knowledge, or skills, but changing into one's self, informed by the new knowledge and skills.*

Every educational event is movement toward a *metanoia*, the passage of spirit from alienation into a deeper awareness of oneself. A spirited epistemology is based on the belief that all education is directed toward such a transformation.

My doctor in Raleigh is a brilliant internist, a deeply caring personal physician. I gave her a copy of *Learning to Listen, Learning to Teach* (Vella, 1994). This hardworking physician told me that as she read the book she realized for the first time that as a doctor she was meant to be an educator. I shared with her a semantic note: the root of the word *doctor* is the Latin word *docere*, which means "to teach." "I never knew that!" she replied in amazement. That day, she learned more than the root of a word. Such knowing is not value-added information. It is intrinsic to the epistemological phenomenon: knowing anything is an opportunity for metanoia, which is a deeper realization of one's meaning and purpose.

Here's another example. Consider the learning experience of an older adult who comes to a community college to learn how to use a computer. An indolent instructor drones on for two of the course's six sessions about the history of computers and the potential of the Internet. The adult learners never touch a keyboard during those six hours. Unconsciously, they learn how stupid they are compared to this self-styled information systems hero. They feel more and more intimidated by the global system and by the laptop computer in front of them. They know how little they know and how unlikely it is that they will ever master this knowledge and these skills. They do not come back to the rest of the course, for which they have already paid.

Precisely this situation occurred recently here in North Carolina. Without a spirited epistemology, without a moral stance, such educational events occur daily. They are a blasphemy.

When the opportunity for metanoia is missed through indolence or ignorance on the part of instructors, it cannot be regained. When will we as adult educators get angry enough about this abuse to take concerted action? This issue of *New Directions for Adult and Continuing Education* is an effort in the right direction.

Principles and Practices for Adult Educators

How can we be sure that we are using a spirited epistemology, inviting men and women to be Subjects of their own learning? Faithful use of the following principles and practices can help to make you accountable to these learners.

Dialogue. The heart of a spirited epistemology is respect for dialogue. Everything in your design moves toward dialogue as a plant moves toward the sunlight. Dialogue is the guiding principle. This means, however, that a teacher accepts a new role as resource person, not as expert; as guide, not as professor; as mentor, not as instructor; as educator, not as facilitator. Freire's famous phrase, "Only the student can name the moment of the death of the professor," which he said in a conversation on our back porch in Dar es Salaam, Tanzania, in 1962, stands editing here. When I design for dialogue, for accountable learning, I can name the moment of the death of the professor in me. Just as we might eschew the term *facilitator* because we know that education is never facile, so we honor the difficulty involved in the changing role of the professor that is called for when we design for dialogue.

Dialogue does not mean that the educator comes in empty-handed. The substantive content he or she brings is not watered down. A spirited epistemology simply means we design in such a way as to listen to the adult learners' experiences and knowledge base, and to build on that which is known with what is new.

When I teach the Seven Steps of Planning, I realize that all of the adults I am teaching have done some kind of planning. They already have a model. In respect for that experience and knowledge, I ask them to do a simple learning task. I ask the participants at each table to examine seven cards on which are written the Seven Steps of Planning:

- Who: participants and leaders
- Why: the situation
- When: the time frame

- Where: the site
- What: content—skills, knowledge, attitudes
- What for: achievement-based objectives
- How: learning tasks and materials

I then ask each group to put the cards in an appropriate order for designing an adult education event. We then go around the room and examine the order set out at each table.

Such a learning task does a number of exciting things: It gets people working together, arguing, and challenging one another. Everyone brings to the task all of their previous knowledge of planning, and they tell one another story after story to defend their choice of sequence. They laugh and tease one another as they move from table to table, discovering other interpretations. They learn, as Subjects, the Seven Steps of Planning not by applying the theory but by making it. Imagine such a learning task in any adult education course—a medical school course in anatomy, a law school course in torts, a cooking class, a community education event on political organizing.

Dialogue must be designed. Effective dialogue is firmly founded on the competence of the educator and the substantive quality of what he or she is teaching. The first step in respect is that the educator does her or his homework.

All learning involves cognitive, affective, and psychomotor elements. When you design learning tasks for adult learners in order to learn what you are teaching, you always include cognitive, affective, and psychomotor elements. For example, in that keynote address in Vermont mentioned earlier in the chapter, I gave the educators the following learning task: In pairs, walk around and read Lewin's twelve principles recorded on the placards. Select two principles that speak most directly to you in your work as an educator and tell one another why you chose those two. We'll hear a sample.

This task involved obvious psychomotor activity—a gallery walk. It involved the affective in the selection and application of some of Lewin's (1951) theories to the participants' work, and it involved cognitive work in reading, analyzing, and applying all twelve principles.

Respect. This principle guides not only the design of learning and of learning tasks, but also every aspect of educators' encounters with adult learners. We can respect adult learners only when we know something of their context and situation. The practice of doing a learning needs assessment with learners prior to a session is a correlative of this principle of respect.

I recently did a weekend professional development course with a group of teachers from the professional studies department of Tusculum College in Tennessee. The brochure inviting their participation described the course and included a short survey for them to complete and fax to me. The prospective participants included professors from Eastern Tennessee State University as well as from Tusculum College, a professional trainer from a local industry, two recent graduates of Tusculum, and a college vice president.

I could feel the course materials and purpose shifting as I read the list. Then the faxes came in, with their responses to three simple questions:

1. Describe your present work.
2. What are the most common problems you have in designing or teaching adult education sessions?
3. You have seen the program description. What are your expectations of the weekend?

I learned from the responses that I needed to adjust the content and the process just enough to meet the participants' needs.

On the first day, I referred to their problems and expectations, which showed that I respected the participants' and their context. I explicitly noted the slight changes I had made to the program; this was further proof that I had read and indeed studied their responses.

A learning task is a task for learners—usually an open question put to them with the resources they need to respond. It is the practice of accountability, responsibility, and teamwork all in one, as learners engage with new content—theories, skills, and attitudes—to complete a learning task together.

Respect for learners lies in the design of the learning task: Is it well sequenced in relation to the rest of the course? Is it well timed for completion by a small group? Is the product that results immediately useful to the participants? Does the content have a substantive research base or call for significant skills so that learners are challenged to push the envelope?

Knowles (1980) shared some basic concepts that guide adult learning: respect, immediacy, relevance, and the fact that adults use 20 percent of what they hear, 40 percent of what they both hear and see, and 80 percent of what they do. These are all incorporated in an effective learning task that invites learners to do something with what they are learning.

The verbs in a learning task explain the intensity of the work: describe, list, read, circle priority items, analyze, synthesize into a single sentence, make a time line, select, design, compose. These verbs describe what the learners do, not what the teacher does. A spirited epistemology is based on what Dewey (1938) taught years ago: learning is in the deciding and in the doing. Can you see how the learning task is an opportunity for learners to practice being Subjects of their own learning?

Accountability. A spirited epistemology is based on the belief that the teacher, through the learning design, is accountable to the learner. This is an exciting new twist. Adult learners often come to their first courses in a literacy center or a graduate school full of fearful questions: Can I do it? Can

I make it? Can I learn this difficult content? Can I understand the materials? Such fear paralyzes the potential of the adult learner.

To demonstrate accountability, use a *learning covenant*. The achievement-based objectives of such a covenant are the backbone of a design that shows exactly what will be taught and learned, and what the learners will do to show themselves that they know what has been taught. In the title of a book I coauthored on evaluation, *How Do They Know They Know?* (Vella, Berardinelli, and Burrow, 1998), the operative word is *they*. Go back and look at the objectives I presented early in this chapter. This was my covenant with you. Has it helped you to learn about a spirited epistemology as you read?

Achievement-based objectives are grounded in the assumption that adult learners want to learn and are willing to do the work involved. Such objectives focus the learning event. They become learning tasks in a sound design. They assure the learner of the educator's accountability to complete the covenant. They make the words *spirited epistemology* become flesh in a time frame, with a tangible product that gives proof of the learning that took place.

A spirited epistemology is not only an attitude. It is also a process, materials, and actions. It involves mutuality of respect and joy in learning. When a teacher is using another epistemology, he or she is not accountable to the learners. Learning is either a spirited partnership or domination.

We cannot overcome the domination system that has prevailed in education for centuries without humor and wit. Walter Wink (1991) tells a story of South African women "teaching" White South African soldiers how precious the women's homes were and how powerful these defenseless homesteaders actually were. Before the end of apartheid, the army was sent to ravage villages where there were no men (they were all in the mines or in cities). At one village the women decided to use what they knew of the background of these White South African soldiers, who were all dutiful Dutch Calvinists. The women met the army at the gate of their village undressed. The army retreated as fast as they could, with their eyes closed. This is use of a spirited epistemology: nonviolent and efficacious.

We need to learn to use our wit, our humor, and our ingenuity to design for dialogue and accountability, for effective learning.

Inviting a Moral Stance from the Adult Learner. This epistemology demands a new relationship between teacher and learner—a relationship of partners in learning, who work together to advance the learning of each partner. My friend and colleague Sarah Gravett (Gravett and Henning, 1998), in South Africa, describes this relationship thus: Based on Mikhail Bakhtin's (1981) theory—which implies that teacher, learner, and knowledge are in a dynamic, reciprocal unity—dialogic teaching is proposed as transformative exchange, in which teachers and learners are involved in a co-learning and co-teaching process, thereby cultivating the development of an authentic community of learners, characterized by sharing and support, along with cognitive challenge.

Demands and Support. This kind of relationship and this sort of spirited epistemology calls for a new preparation for educators, and a way of bringing those presently engaged in education to a new way of designing curricula, designing courses, and teaching. The seminal work of Dewey (1938), Freire (1970), Bakhtin (1981), Rogers (1961), and Knowles (1980) continue to move us forward and nudge the revolution in education. The desperation of students leaving school in droves at sixteen to get minimum-wage jobs and buy a secondhand car on credit urges us to develop a new system of relevant education. The pleas of industry, government, and health services for creative, critical thinkers makes this effort vital (Senge, 1990).

The Future of Such an Approach

Donald Oliver (1989) distinguishes between technical and ontological knowing. Technical knowing is information or a set of directions for developing a skill. Memorizing a time line of events leading to the Vietnam war is technical knowing. Practicing how to send and store electronic mail is technical knowing. Ontological knowing is analyzing world events to determine cause—media, statesmen, politicians, the military, local culture, or religion. Ontology is the study of being. Ontological knowing has to do with being human, being men and being women, being society. Considering the potential of e-mail, testing mass deliveries and analyzing their effect is ontological knowing. Both types of knowing are necessary and both need a spirited epistemology. Reverence here lies in the distinction between the two. How can my work with an adult learner in a literacy course become ontological knowing? How do I design a staff meeting so that the learning involved is not only technical but also ontological? This is what we are aiming at by inviting a spirited epistemology.

It is time for this spiritual revolution. How we educate one another and our children is a symbol of our society. At the beginning of the twentieth century, Dewey recognized that education was designed to prepare women and men for factory jobs on an assembly line or for soldiering. A spirited epistemology is not designed for that purpose. The twenty-first century invites men and women in industry, in the military, in agriculture or government, in the church or the media, in health care or in international development to be creative, critical thinkers who feel certain that their suggestions will be heard. Democracy is a real option now. Unless we teach one another as spiritual, human beings, we will continue to feed a domination system that will be our death. A spirited epistemology is appropriate not only in adult education but in any educational effort.

This is our choice. This is our moral stance. In the chapter that follows, Linda Vogel builds on this chapter by focusing on adult educators and what it means for them to reckon with their spiritual lives. The following chapters in this volume offer distinct and specific ways to implement such a choice in a number of settings. We move forward in hope, knowing that we know how to use a spirited epistemology, because we just did so.

References

Bakhtin, M. M. *The Dialogic Imagination: Four Essays.* Austin: University of Texas Press, 1981.
Dewey, J. *Experience and Education.* Old Tappan, N.J.: Macmillan, 1938.
Freire, P. *Pedagogy of the Oppressed.* New York: Continuum, 1970.
Gravett, S., and Henning, E. "Dialogic Epistemology for Instructional Design." Unpublished paper. Johannesburg, South Africa: Faculty of Education, Afrikaans University, 1998.
Johnson, D. W., and Johnson, F. *Joining Together.* Englewood Cliffs, N.J.: Prentice Hall, 1987.
Knowles, M. *The Modern Practice of Adult Education: From Pedagogy to Andragogy.* (2nd ed.) Chicago: Follett, 1980. (Originally published 1970)
Lewin, K. *Field Theory in Social Science.* New York: HarperCollins, 1951.
Oliver, D. W., with Gershman, K. W. *Education, Modernity, and Fractured Meaning: Toward a Process Theory of Teaching and Learning.* New York: State University of New York Press, 1989.
Rogers, C. R. *On Becoming a Person: A Therapist's View of Psychotherapy.* Boston: Houghton Mifflin, 1961.
Senge, P. M. *The Fifth Discipline: The Art and Practice of the Learning Organization.* New York: Doubleday, 1990.
Vella, J. *Learning to Listen, Learning to Teach: The Power of Dialogue in Educating Adults.* San Francisco: Jossey-Bass, 1994.
Vella, J., Berardinelli, P., and Burrow, J. *How Do They Know They Know? Evaluating Adult Learning.* San Francisco: Jossey-Bass, 1998.
Wink, W. *Engaging the Powers.* Minneapolis: Augsburg Fortress, 1991.

JANE VELLA is founder and chair of the board of Global Learning Partners, Inc., a consulting and training company based in Raleigh, North Carolina.

2

Teaching and learning that are holistic must be open to and reckon with the spiritual lives of both adult educators and learners; educators must design processes that invite the involvement of whole persons while honoring the experience of each person in ways that leave room for diversity and mystery.

Reckoning with the Spiritual Lives of Adult Educators

Linda J. Vogel

As we embark on a new millennium, we find ourselves in a world full of pain, anger, and mistrust. Some people claim to have all the answers. Others have given up hope and opted out. Still others acknowledge that there are multiple sources from which persons can seek meaning.

People have different priorities and different lenses through which they view life and the world. There are multiple communities with differing values and assumptions. We, as adult educators, recognize that there are multiple intelligences and that if we are to teach adults and learn with them, they must be addressed as whole persons and invited to bring their life experiences and questions to a safe table where all are given voice and can be heard.

Adult educators seeking to teach with truth and integrity need to bring their whole selves into dialogue not only with the subject matter but also with the learners (Subjects, as in Chapter One), who are also whole persons. Our spirits—our inner lives, our hearts—affect who we are and how we engage others and the world. The stories and rituals of our families and faith communities have helped us become who we are as persons.

Spiritual Threads of Our Lives

Defining *spirituality* is a nebulous task; there is no commonly agreed-upon definition. Some find the term to their liking; others find it too vague and without substance. Some feel that the word *spirituality* diminishes their religious faith, whatever it might be; for others it is a preferred term precisely because it does not contain particular doctrinal, historical, or theological content.

A yearning toward light and wholeness leads many adult educators toward rituals, common stories of faith and hope, symbols and images, and a sense that there is more to life than who we are or can ever be. When we are drawn to visions of justice, compassion, righteousness, and peace, we embrace more than the material and mundane, or the here and now.

When we stand on a threshold, we dare to move out of a past that has formed us into a future that beckons us to step beyond what we know into a new space and time. We grasp the truth that past, present, and future are interwoven in a myriad of ways. Reflecting on how our past informs us in the present and propels us toward an unknown future helps us stay rooted. We can bloom where we are planted and imagine ourselves in gardens yet to be created.

As we discover connecting threads that bind generation with generation, and faith with everyday life, we create possibilities for seeing with new eyes and hearing beyond the blaring noises of a hurting world. As we reckon with our spiritual lives, we encounter, reflect, imagine, and create different ways of seeing and engaging persons and situations with renewed energy, hope, and vision.

The Content of Our Spiritual Lives

No matter what family and faith tradition we grew up in (mine was Christian, United Methodist), there are stories and dreams, hopes and fears, gifts and wounds that make us who we are. This is true whether we grew up in a church, synagogue, mosque, temple, or shrine and still claim it as home, or if we reject past family or religious experience as no longer home. Some of us may never have participated in a religious community or tradition. The metaphors, stories, songs, and rituals that adult educators (and learners, too) carry inform how they understand gift and obligation, gratitude and service, hope and fear, trust and shame, love and punishment.

Our spiritual lives reflect the dreams, fears, and commitments out of which we live, work, play, and pray. When we claim our spiritual selves and take responsibility for understanding and nurturing the spiritual dimension of our being, we learn to teach with a deeper sense of who we are, and to embody integrity in powerful, vulnerable ways.

Lawyer Stephen Carter (1996) suggests that if we are to live and interact as persons of integrity, and to build an ethical society, then all persons must engage in the hard work of discerning right and wrong. We must invite those who journey with us to enter into this process of discernment. Knowing right from wrong is never enough. We must act on that knowing—even if it costs us something. Finally, doing right is not enough; we must name what we are doing and why—offering it up for public witness and scrutiny.

Inviting adult learners to explore connections between their own spiritual lives and integrity is vital. Helping these learners explore what it means to embody integrity in committed relationships, families, business dealings, social relationships, faith communities, and government brings both responsibility and challenge if an adult educator is to teach in holistic ways.

Adult educators who are open to diversity and who acknowledge a spirited epistemology leave room for mystery. They can guide adults into critical and creative reflection by modeling clarity, consistency, openness, communicativeness, specificity, and accessibility (Brookfield, 1988).

Parker Palmer (1998) is right when he asserts that "good teachers join self and subject and students in the fabric of life" (p. 11). When our "self" is whole—body, mind, will, and spirit—the gift we bring to our subject matter and our students is filled with potential for understanding more deeply and engaging more fully. This openness and vulnerability fosters transforming and life-giving teaching.

Acknowledging and Seeking to Heal Spiritual Wounds

There can be no doubt that many persons have been victimized and seriously wounded in the name of God or some divine authority and at the hand of religious institutions. To deny or ignore the spiritual aspects of our lives cannot remedy this reality. Rather, to name the abuses and misuses of religious power and to address them directly is the appropriate and necessary response.

I remember talking with a retired CEO after a book discussion in his church. The group had wrestled vigorously for more than two hours on a Saturday morning about issues of faith and science as reflected in the book they were reading. The CEO said, "This is the first church I've found where you don't have to check your mind and your sense of humor at the door!" He was thankful that he had found such a church. But we must not fall into the reverse trap. Persons should never feel that they need to check their faith and their religious commitments and questions at any door: church, classroom, work, or home. Bringing our whole being to all our experiences should be the norm for learning, both inside faith communities and in the larger worlds of work and leisure.

Roberta Bondi (1995) calls on persons of faith to envision thinking and talking about God (or that which is beyond human experience) in ways that are life-giving. A logical extension of this idea is that as persons seek to engage the spiritual, they must discern false images and beliefs that are destructive rather than life-giving. Images that bind rather than liberate need to be rooted out. Seeking a spiritual path must lead toward healing and wholeness—toward an affirmation of self, others, and the whole universe.

As persons seek to become whole, their ways of being and relating have the potential to be transformed so that the persons are truer to who they are and to who they are becoming. This shift releases them so that they can be open to and accepting of others. When persons are able to embrace all that they are—claiming gifts, naming wounds, and owning questions—there is a greater freedom to be present for others as well. To reckon with our spiritual selves requires that we look both inward and outward—engaging the wounds and seeking the healing that can lead to wholeness.

Commitment to the Common Good in a Complex World

The authors of *Common Fire* (Daloz, Keen, Keen, and Parks, 1996) describe common factors present in families of adults who were able to sustain commitment to the common good over time. These families provided "a safe environment" that offered "shelter and nourishment" with "at least one trustworthy adult." There was "time and space to express and heal the inevitable pain and hurt of life" (p. 219). When these factors are present in adult learners, teaching is greatly enhanced. When they are not, adult educators need to create safe and shameless space where learners are free to grow toward wholeness.

Teachers and mentors of adult learners increase their effectiveness when they hold *challenge* and *support* in creative tension so that learners feel safe enough to risk examining assumptions and entertaining some alternate possibilities for ways to do and be. The art of teaching is knowing when and how to support and when and how to challenge adult learners. Holding persons within boundaries helps them stay with the tough issues under consideration. When teachers are in touch with their own spiritual journeys, they engage learners in ways that encourage them to explore all dimensions of a topic. Recognition that spirituality permeates one's entire being makes compartmentalization of the various aspects of learning a less viable way of engaging subject matter and students. How teachers listen to students and are vulnerable with them serves as a model for bringing the whole self to the table. This is true whether the subject matter is studying a current novel, designing a new organizational structure for a corporation, or confronting moral decisions.

A law partner needs to bring into meetings with her partners her commitment to represent her clients in the best possible way, to bill fairly, and to have quality time with her children. When we take our whole being seriously—including our spirituality—we are not able to leave family concerns out of the boardroom, or concerns for integrity and justice out of family relationships.

Connecting the Ordinary and the Sacred

Many writers suggest that the sacred is present in the ordinariness of everyday living. The experience of *place* can help us ground our spirituality (see Bender, 1995; Brussat and Brussat, 1996; Norris, 1993). We are called to recognize that everyday tasks such as baking bread, bathing babies, and mowing yards can be spiritual acts. Lighting candles, walking in the woods, watching children play on a crowded city sidewalk, and sitting in a darkened room can be openings to the holy.

Thomas Bender asserts that our acts of "holding sacred" are at our core; in such acts we give places power to affect our lives (1991, p. 324). By becoming attuned to our special place or places and to the power of place in our lives, we are better able to see and acknowledge all our connections.

The subtitle of Kathleen Norris's (1993) book *Dakota: A Spiritual Geography* both reflects and generates metaphors such as *landscapes* and *home*. Likewise, our heart, or our "inmost being," is often seen as a sacred place. Place making becomes a spiritual discipline as persons find places to be "at home."

Ruth Duck's hymn "Lead On, O Cloud of Presence" provided Nelle Morton (1985) with the title for her book *The Journey Is Home*. This phrase links home and journey in powerful ways. In this day of high mobility and constant change, finding ways to embrace life's journey as our home can offer both roots and wings to those who teach. We need not always long for more, bigger, and better things, or for a future that never seems to come. When we embrace each day as home, we may become less driven and more able to experience our connections with all of life.

Reckoning with our own spiritual lives can be life-giving and may help adult educators find ways to invite students to reckon with their spiritual lives. This is an awesome responsibility that holds potential for transformative teaching and learning. Once we open the door to talking about beliefs and the practices of faith, we are called to listen in deep, open ways and to recognize that sharing faith can be done noncoercively so that we are able to understand and honor different experiences and beliefs. Adult educators who invite learners into such a journey may help them think metaphorically about place and home.

Adult educators can think about ways this might be done at a political campaign strategy meeting, at a meeting of the board of directors of a hospital, or during a continuing education event for retail business employees. This approach gives rise to a number of questions: Can home be both the day-to-day journey and the place toward which we are journeying? Can all that persons think, feel, and do be seen as homemaking? How does what adults seek to learn help them be intentional about their journeys and their homecomings?

Strategies for Reckoning with Our Spiritual Lives

Moving toward more holistic ways of engaging adults in education means creating safe and hospitable space "where obedience to truth is practiced" (Palmer, 1983, p. 69). As Vella says in Chapter One, respecting the Subject-learner means that teachers listen, begin where learners are, and dialogue in ways that recognize boundaries and hold all participants accountable. At the same time, teachers invite learners to risk by exploring ideas and issues creatively and imaginatively.

Offering hospitality that is genuine and truthful and that creates room for deep and frank dialogue and disagreement is one of the first tasks for fostering holistic teaching and learning. It requires recognizing that ambiguity and complexity exist in all situations and that differences are real.

Adult educators often choose to interact with folks who look and think like they do, therefore reducing ambiguity. But this choice leads inevitably to myopic vision that fails to see from many different perspectives. It does little to help adults function and contribute in a world that is increasingly diverse.

As adult educators we can both challenge and support persons on their journeys toward truth and wholeness by learning to reframe questions. Let me give an example. When we ask, "Is this theory true?" persons may be quick to choose sides and defend the conclusion that the theory is either true or not true. When we change the question to, "What truth is there in this theory that may help us address our problem?" a whole new way of engaging the material is opened up.

There is a temptation to steer clear of issues or problems that we know people have strong feelings and disagreements about. Often, however, these issues are vitally important to individuals and communities. This conclusion begs the question: Is there a better alternative?

Finding ways to facilitate the naming and facing of conflict in fair and nonjudgmental ways is another way that adult educators can help learners face life-giving and life-denying issues that keep folks awake at night. What does one believe about ending life (assisted suicide, euthanasia, abortion, murder, capital punishment)? The way we name an issue matters. The words we choose can raise anxiety and foster fear and anger, or they can be more descriptive and less inflammatory. What happens when we frame the issue by creating a continuum that places the sanctity of life at one pole and the quality of life at the other? This approach invites persons to look at a wide range of possible options and to consider particular circumstances in particular contexts. They are not forced to be pro-life or pro-choice; rather, they can begin to talk about the various criteria that must be examined. For example, how they view capital punishment not only involves what they believe about taking human life, but also addresses how they protect other human lives and society in general. It invites them to examine attitudes and beliefs about retribution and rehabilitation.

What happens when we look at all the different and sometimes conflicting beliefs and values we hold? Usually we begin to talk about what we believe, about what factors have higher priority for us and why. It becomes safe to talk about the questions our own positions raise for us. When we engage others in order to understand better their commitments and decisions, rather than to persuade them to believe as we do, there is the potential for everyone to gain a better understanding of the issues. When our goal is to clarify and understand our beliefs, we sometimes find our positions shifting. When we are committed to safe and hospitable space where true dialogue can occur, it becomes possible to engage even the most controversial issues in ways that are respectful. Adults can learn to agree to disagree in respectful ways that do not attack the value or integrity of others whose deeply held values may be different.

John Cobb (1993) helps persons who seek to be attuned to the spiritual aspects of life examine their beliefs. His process requires them to bring their religious beliefs to a level of awareness and then view them in relation to their other beliefs. In this way, they may seek to justify their beliefs on the basis of their own faith tradition and commitments. This process helps them to look long and hard at the assumptions underlying their beliefs. By asking what the source of those beliefs is, persons can begin to see whether, in fact, they come from somewhere other than their faith tradition. Upon examination, many beliefs that we assume come from our faith tradition actually come from our family of origin, our culture, our social class, or our fears.

For example, some persons may have been taught that women or Christians or Asians must keep the peace (that is, not express anger, suppress their own needs and desires in order to soothe troubled waters, and so on). Although this socialization may have been based on religious or filial or gender values, when we look for the root source, we may find that this attitude is the way a dominant group maintains power and control over other groups.

This process for examining our beliefs is valid for persons from any faith tradition as well as for those with no tradition at all. The key is to help people name what they believe, to look at why they believe what they claim to believe and how their beliefs connect with one another. They can then be invited to examine the assumptions that underlie their beliefs, and seek to identify the real and varied sources on which these assumptions rest. This can be an eye-opening experience.

Let me offer an example from bell hooks (1994), one that I apply to my own teaching. Her chapter "Confronting Class in the Classroom" made me aware that some of my assumptions about the place of conflict and appropriate expressions of conflict in the classroom grew out of my own white, middle-class, female expectations and assumptions. I discovered that my discomfort with students interrupting rather than waiting silently to be called on in teaching and learning settings is culturally based and not a prerequisite for inherently good teaching and learning.

Examining the Content of Teaching

At this point, I need to say a word about the subject matter or content of teaching, because it too has a voice of its own. In addition to seeing learners as Subjects, as Vella does in Chapter One, we need to recognize that the content (also subject) is the third leg of the adult education stool. One of the dangers in adult education is that teachers assume that their voice is the content's voice—that teachers and what they teach are one. All content has a voice of its own. The teacher's role is to be resource, guide, and facilitator—to present the subject fairly and invite students to reflect on, question, and engage the subject.

Adult educators can introduce students to concepts and skills. They can frame questions and provide teaching strategies that can lead students into the subject at hand. To teach is to offer constructive critique, to urge learners to go deeper and cast their nets further. It is to entice them to follow some leads that branch off the main road, to introduce new vocabulary, a provocative metaphor, or different ways of categorizing data.

Belenky, Clinchy, Goldberger, and Tarule (1986) describe the teacher's role as "midwife." Harris (1988) also builds on this image to offer us a powerful example that relies on a strong sense of community. She explains that the fate of the Jewish people depended on midwives who dared to stand against the Pharaoh's order that all Hebrew infant boys be killed. The midwives chose life over death for the good of the community, regardless of the consequences for themselves.

Adult educators as midwives assist other people in giving birth to new ideas, new skills, new metaphors, and new ways of being and doing. They assist learners in giving birth to their own ideas, visions, and goals. They bring their knowledge and skills in teaching and offer them to the students with whom they learn.

If adult educators find that learners are mirroring the educators' beliefs and actions, painting in the same style, copying their way of relating in the workplace or discoursing in a court of law, then it is time for those adult educators to examine what they are doing. The role of midwife educators is not to replicate themselves. Rather, the midwife is a representative of a community that fosters knowledge, values, creativity, and growth in all its members. Teaching becomes steps in a dance that circles around so that the steps of the dance are created and recreated by those who dance the dance (Harris, 1988).

Teaching is about engaging in a connective process that embodies both "stance and dance" (Brookfield, 1995, p. 42). It plays itself out in a rhythm that pulses among engaging knowledge, exploring alternative ways of thinking and acting, developing autonomy, and fostering interdependence. This dance strives toward and creates mutually held visions that empower rather than enslave, stretch rather than stifle, honor diversity rather than homogeneity, and seek always to be acts of integrity.

Donald Schön (1987, p. 41) refers to "the architectural studio" as a metaphor for what he calls a "reflection-in-action" model for teaching and learning. Teachers need to devise processes to assist learners as they engage a question, issue, or topic; make connections; examine assumptions; explore alternative ways of addressing a problem or subject; and work together to create new ways of knowing and doing.

As Palmer (1983) asserts when he dares to write about "a spirituality of education," "the teacher, like any lover, must be capable of having a lover's quarrel with the subject, stretching and testing the loved one and the relation-ship" (p. 104). When adult educators dare to ask hard questions, reframe questions so that everyone has to engage them from many different angles, and encourage learners to look at the assumptions underlying their own beliefs, both teachers and learners cannot avoid reckoning with their own spiritual lives. Whenever adults risk going to the core of their beliefs, they are apt to come face to face with the resources and wounds that are embedded in their spiritual selves. Growth and transformation become possible whenever adults connect their daily lives to their spiritual homes, that place where they grow toward wholeness.

The call to adult educators that requires that they be challenged by and that they challenge adult learners to explore and explode boundaries and presuppositions that limit or impede growth is a call to transformative teaching and learning. It asks those who teach to risk, because no educator has a right to ask adult learners to do what the educator himself or herself is unwilling to do.

Strategies for Fostering Spiritual Growth

There are a wide variety of strategies for fostering holistic ways of thinking critically and imaginatively in adults. These strategies include working together on critical incidents or case studies, journaling, and using contemporary film and literature (an increasing number of best-selling books—both fiction and nonfiction—include discussion guides for use with small groups).

Oprah's Book Club and the YaYa Sisterhoods are two examples of the interest and power that adults are finding in reading and discussing issues that touch their lives. Looking critically at the media and advertising and seeking to name the assumptions out of which they operate can be eye-opening. It can lead to an examination of personal and institutional or corporate assumptions. Using creative activities such as art, drama, and music can also foster new ways of looking at and connecting our affective and cognitive responses (see Mezirow and Associates, 1991).

Adult educators need to engage in what Christensen, Garvin, and Sweet (1991) refer to as the "instant artistry" of living within a triad that consists of framing questions (tone is always more crucial than words!) that invite, engage, and challenge learners; fostering deep and attentive listening; and choosing to respond so that the group explores further, extends beyond, or pushes deeper while avoiding tangents and continuing to wrestle with life's complexities.

Collaborative ways of engaging in reflection-action-reflection models of problem solving are being used in corporations, colleges and universities, business, and government. When our theoretical assumptions and frameworks inform our actions, and our actions modify our theories so that future actions grow out of what we have learned by experience and critical and creative reflection, the whole system is energized. A spiral is created that is good for institutions and business, for products and services, and for those who work in these systems.

This approach does not impose any faith tradition or particular beliefs on learners. Space is neither safe nor hospitable if it does not honor diverse voices and protect the right of all persons to take responsibility for what they will share and for their own learning. Daloz (1999, pp. 203–229) uses a wonderful phrase when he encourages teachers of adults to invite students "to let air under your assumptions." It is not life threatening to ask persons to "suppose that" or to play with "what if." Teachers and mentors of adults are sometimes called to "heat up dichotomies," which is somewhat more challenging than playing with "what if." Often it is the adult educator's role to "hold up a mirror" so that all in the learning community are able to see for themselves. In Chapter Three of this volume, Leona English highlights the role of mentors in the continuous education of adults.

Many adults find ways of being and doing in the world without naming mystery at all—though few in the United States and Canada are untouched by the faith stories and traditions that permeate Western Judeo-Christian culture. Those who come from other lands bring at least the vestiges of Christian colonizers; of Shintoism, Confucianism, Buddhism, Hinduism, or Islam; or of beliefs that have grown out of the religious practices of native peoples or other religious traditions.

We have been looking at what it means for adult educators to reckon with their own spirituality as they teach and learn with adults. When adult educators invite learners to journey toward wholeness by entering into a "spirited epistemology" (see Chapter One of this volume) that seeks a more just and compassionate way of being in the world, horizons are expanded and all are invited to share in the benefits of that work.

Teaching as whole persons who reckon with their own spirituality becomes an act of caring. The relationship between subject matter and learners is a gift requiring deep respect. Whenever adult educators seek to foster attentiveness to both mind and heart in themselves and others, they are walking on holy ground (Vogel, 1991). Reckoning with their spiritual lives calls teachers to live sacramentally—to be open to mystery and willing to "color outside the lines," as the subtitle of my book suggests (Vogel and Vogel, 1999).

References

Belenky, M. F., Clinchy, B. M., Goldberger, N. R., and Tarule, J. M. *Women's Ways of Knowing: The Development of Self, Voice, and Mind.* New York: Basic Books, 1986. .

Bender, S. *Everyday Sacred: A Woman's Journey Home.* San Francisco: Harper San Francisco, 1995.

Bender, T. "Making Places Sacred." In J. Swan (ed.), *Power of Place.* Wheaton, Il.: Quest, 1991.

Bondi, R. C. *Memories of God: Theological Reflections on a Life.* Nashville, Tenn.: Abingdon Press, 1995.

Brookfield, S. D. *Developing Critical Thinkers: Challenging Adults to Explore Alternative Ways of Thinking and Acting.* San Francisco: Jossey-Bass, 1988.

Brookfield, S. D. *Becoming a Critically Reflective Teacher.* San Francisco: Jossey-Bass, 1995.

Brussat, F., and Brussat, M. A. *Spiritual Literacy: Reading the Sacred in Everyday Life.* New York: Scribner, 1996.

Carter, S. L. *Integrity.* New York: HarperCollins, 1996.

Christensen, C. R., Garvin, D. A., and Sweet, A. *Education for Judgment: The Artistry of Discussion Leadership.* Boston, Mass.: Harvard Business School Press, 1991.

Cobb, J. B., Jr. *Becoming a Thinking Christian.* Nashville, Tenn.: Abingdon Press, 1993.

Daloz, L. A. *Mentor: Guiding the Journey of Adult Learners.* (2nd ed.). San Francisco: Jossey-Bass, 1999.

Daloz, L.A.P., Keen, C. H., Keen, J. P., and Parks, S. D. *Common Fire: Lives of Commitment in a Complex World.* Boston: Beacon Press, 1996.

Harris, M. *Women and Teaching: Themes for a Spirituality of Pedagogy.* Mahwah, N.J.: Paulist Press, 1988.

hooks, b. *Teaching to Transgress: Education as the Practice of Freedom.* New York: Routledge, 1994.

Mezirow J., and Associates. *Fostering Critical Reflection in Adulthood: A Guide to Transformative and Emancipatory Learning.* San Francisco: Jossey-Bass, 1991.

Morton, N. *The Journey Is Home.* Boston: Beacon Press, 1985.

Norris, K. *Dakota: A Spiritual Geography.* New York: Ticknor & Fields, 1993.

Palmer, P. J. *To Know as We Are Known: A Spirituality of Education.* San Francisco: Harper San Francisco, 1983.

Palmer, P. J. *The Courage to Teach: Exploring the Inner Landscape of a Teacher's Life.* San Francisco: Jossey-Bass, 1998.

Schön, D. A. *Educating the Reflective Practitioner.* San Francisco: Jossey-Bass, 1987.

Vogel, D. W., and Vogel, L. J. *Sacramental Living: Falling Stars and Coloring Outside the Lines.* Nashville, Tenn.: Upper Room Books, 1999.

Vogel, L. J. *Teaching and Learning in Communities of Faith: Empowering Adults Through Religious Education.* San Francisco: Jossey-Bass, 1991.

LINDA J. VOGEL *is professor of Christian Education at Garrett-Evangelical Theological Seminary, Evanston, Illinois, and a deacon in full connection in the United Methodist Church.*

3

This chapter describes three cases in which the informal learning strategies of mentoring, self-directed learning, and dialogue have been used to facilitate spiritual development.

Spiritual Dimensions of Informal Learning

Leona M. English

One of the primary insights of adult education is that informal and incidental learning occur continuously in the everyday world, spurring reflection on people's actions and cultivating individual and group learning and development (Watkins and Marsick, 1992). In this chapter, I focus on three primary informal learning strategies: mentoring, self-directed learning (SDL), and dialogue. I explore how each of these strategies can facilitate spiritual development in distinct but sometimes overlapping ways. I highlight these informal learning practices as untapped sources that contribute to the spiritual development of adults, and provide further insights into the dynamics of their learning.

Although I isolate the spiritual dimension of learning, I realize that the boundaries and distinctions between the various dimensions of learning are in reality seamless, and that the whole of learning embraces the cognitive, spiritual, social, emotional, physical, and affective dimensions. I am also aware that although I present mentoring, SDL, and dialogue in a positive light, each has the potential to foster learning that is not life affirming (Ervin, 1995).

Aspects of Spirituality

As early as 1925, British educator Basil Yeaxlee wrote extensively on the need to recognize the spiritual dimensions of adult education, which he equated with religion. Almost seventy-five years later, my concerns are similar, although my understanding of spirituality is broader than Yeaxlee's. In this chapter, I examine three components of authentic spiritual development

New Directions for Adult and Continuing Education, no. 85, Spring 2000 © Jossey-Bass Publishers

that relate to adult learning and that informal learning can foster: a strong sense of self; care, concern, and outreach to others; and the continuous construction of meaning and knowledge:

- *Strong sense of self.* While adults are learning, they frequently benefit from relationships with other people, especially from those that are safe and supportive. Adults learn from their encounters with others about alternate and varied ways of being, and they acquire new insights about themselves. In forming and maintaining relationships, adults are provided with an opportunity to learn about their deepest longings and desires; in relationships they develop a stronger sense of self, which is integral to spiritual development. As MacKeracher (1996) observes, spirituality develops from a strong sense of self, without which "we would have little inclination to move out into the world" (p. 164).

- *Care, concern, and outreach to others.* These are integral aspects of authentic spirituality (English, 1999a). A fully integrated spiritual person reaches beyond his or her self and acknowledges the interdependence of all of creation, appreciates the uniqueness of others, and ultimately assumes responsibility for caring and being concerned about other humans and the natural order. Human life is enhanced when adults acknowledge the possibility of drawing strength from others, learning from them, and appreciating their presence as life-giving and affirming. This recognition is consistent with Schneiders's (1986) description of spirituality as "self-transcendence toward the ultimate value one perceives" (p. 266).

- *The continuous construction of meaning and knowledge.* The constantly evolving opportunity to engage with others and in the activities in which one is involved assists in the process of constructing meaning from experience (Merriam and Heuer, 1996). The search for meaning is bound up in the understanding of everyday life. It involves a realization that life is greater than our sphere of influence and that our future is bound up with that of others. The opportunity to find relevance and meaning, to be part of something beyond ourselves, is profoundly spiritual.

Strategies That Foster Spiritual Development

Although not all informal learning strategies foster spiritual development, I believe that mentoring, SDL, and dialoguing have the potential to foster each of the various components of spiritual development. I agree with Watkins and Marsick (1992) that effective adult educators promote informal learning strategies, and that in the process they can also work toward increasing opportunities for spiritual growth.

Mentoring. Mentoring is the personal and professional assistance that one adult (the mentor) provides to another, less experienced adult (the mentee). Mentorship is the interpersonal relationship that occurs between two individuals that provides the potential for them to "be and to become"

(English, 1998). Mentorship can occur in classrooms, in informal situations, in churches, among practitioners—anywhere that an adult is in need of being taught, sponsored, guided, counseled, and befriended by someone who is more experienced. Mentorship is a complex yet informal system of learning, initiation, and ongoing support that encompasses career and psychosocial support (Kram, 1983).

According to Levinson (1978), the writer who popularized the notion of mentoring in adult education, a mentor is one who helps in realizing their life aspirations. In a similar vein, Daloz (1986) has described the mentor as a guide and companion. Elsewhere, the mentor is portrayed as an informal teacher who shows the way and provides the mentee with knowledge and skills (English, 1998). Mentorship transcends the competition and negativity that often sully the learning environment, by fostering and affirming informal learning relationships that promote growth and change. In the next chapter, Wickett also explores mentorship in a spiritual context.

Gehrke (1988b) describes mentoring as a gift exchange and as an I-Thou relationship (1988a) in which the mentor hallows the mentee and vice versa. For Gehrke, mentorship is a spiritual practice or discipline that "holds up" the other as a subject for care, respect, and concern. It is the emptying out of one into the other. Similarly, from a Jewish perspective, Zeldin (1995) claims that the hallmarks of mentoring are reciprocity and mutual respect. For Zeldin, mentorship is an informal relationship in which one person genuinely respects the other. In practice, such reciprocity and respect presuppose that although one may know more about some things than others do, everyone has life experiences to share.

To illustrate this strategy, I use the example of the Antigonish Movement. It began in eastern Nova Scotia at St. Francis Xavier University and was predicated on informal learning, particularly on mentorship. The giants of this social reform movement, Moses Coady and Jimmy Tompkins (Gillen, 1998; Lotz and Welton, 1997), used informal learning strategies such as mentoring because they understood that person-to-person contact was vital for encouraging the growth of their social movement. Lotz and Welton, for instance, note that one of Tompkins's strategies was to pick out the "little fellows . . . and to encourage them to make the best use of their abilities. He would support them, but he would also expect these able people to find solutions for themselves and for their families" (p. 101). Tompkins, Coady, and their coworkers distributed pamphlets, held town hall meetings, and encouraged local farmers, fishers, and coal miners until they gained the self-determination necessary to start their own farming, fishing, grocery, and housing cooperatives. In Chapter Seven, Wilf Bean explores the spiritual basis of the Antigonish Movement from a different perspective.

Strong Sense of Self. The Antigonish Movement was able to succeed because the leaders engendered a strong sense of self among the people. Coady and Tompkins were the force behind the "little fellow," saying "Yes, you can" when spirits were low and worker autonomy seemed impossible.

These leaders understood that human potential requires nurturing and that the best way to nurture it is by building self-confidence and sponsoring intentional learning activities such as study circles. Ultimately, a belief in people and the conviction that they could be rulers of their own destiny was key in making this social and economic movement effective.

Care, Concern, and Outreach to the Other. Another hallmark of this social reform endeavor was the leaders' belief that mentoring was part of their own social responsibility. Tompkins and Coady both could have opted for the simple, uncomplicated life enjoyed by some of their peers. Instead, they chose the challenging task of mentoring a group of people who had the potential to reverse the fortunes of eastern Nova Scotians. They believed that there was no other viable economic route for these people, so they promoted the cooperative movement, which was premised on mutual benefits, social support, and a better life for all—principles that grounded the mentoring practices of the leaders and their field-workers.

Continuous Construction of Meaning and Knowledge. The conviction of the leaders that they did not have ready-made answers for the people of Nova Scotia was a key aspect of the mentoring process during the Antigonish Movement's golden age. Rather, the leaders saw their task as nurturing and kindling the fires of justice in others. Tompkins and Coady challenged miners, farmers, and fishers to create their own dreams of cooperative economic activity and of increased educational achievement. They engaged farmers, fishers, and miners in study groups and town meetings in which participants critiqued their work lives, examined alternative possibilities, and made strides toward cooperative activity. The ideals that undergirded the Antigonish Movement—to enable people to see beyond themselves and reach for greater independence—are essentially those of all adult education, that is, to help individuals make meaning out of their experiences (Merriam and Heuer, 1996).

Self-Directed Learning. Self-directed learning has considerable untapped potential to foster spiritual development in the learner. The term *self-directed learning* can refer to a multiplicity of phenomena (Candy, 1991). According to Caffarella (1993), SDL includes finding out how to drive a car or how to manage a home without ever taking a course or receiving a diploma. She notes that "the learner chooses to assume the primary responsibility for planning, carrying out and evaluating these learning experiences" (p. 28). Consistent with Candy, Caffarella observes that adults do not necessarily learn alone; rather, they often learn in relationship with others.

Brookfield (1983) also points out that independent learners frequently do not learn by themselves. He notes, for example, that hobbyists often learn from one another. In highlighting the interpersonal dimension of the SDL project, Brookfield points out what many of us know intuitively—that knowledge is constructed collaboratively. Not surprisingly, SDL fosters self-development in the individual (Walker, 1993). SDL is concerned with increasing self-understanding and awareness, which are dimensions of a relevant and growing spirituality that occurs in relationship with others.

To illustrate this strategy, I use an example from my own professional practice. I am a faculty member in a self-directed master of adult education program. Each trimester, a group of twelve adult learners arrives on our campus for an intensive three-week period and begins the process of developing a comprehensive learning plan for their thesis-based master's program. In a group context and in individual tutorial sessions with a faculty member, all twelve learners identify and negotiate what they want to learn and how they are going to learn it; they then design individualized learning plans.

Each learner works on building a support network, connecting with other learners through e-mail and on scheduled weekends, and planning periodic meetings with the faculty advisor. The learner completes the master's program at home, in his or her place of practice. Most of the significant learning in the program occurs informally, through learner-initiated projects, interactions with peers, and rigorous self-assessment. This self-directed master's program challenges the learners, fosters growth, and promotes self-directedness. The spiritual dimension is especially evident in the relationships that develop, in the respect that characterizes the relationship between faculty member and learner, and among learners. The building of mutuality and respect, the stretching to be all one can be, is an explicitly spiritual dimension.

Strong Sense of Self. One of the primary objectives of faculty in this master's program is to help students develop ways to increase their own self-directedness. Faculty encourage informal learning by having learners examine in a journal their own educational practice, their personal learning, and their progress in the program. Learners are encouraged to strengthen and develop a strong and clear sense of self and their own abilities. Many graduates who go on for further study choose equally fluid, self-directed programs instead of traditional course-based programs. Graduates report confidence in their own academic ability, the capacity to learn informally from their everyday practice, and willingness to reflect critically on their own learning.

Care, Concern, and Outreach to Others. In this master's program, adult education practitioners are expected to engage in action-oriented projects in their respective workplaces. Most of all, learners are asked to identify and complete projects in which they have a personal interest. They invariably select projects that reflect their commitment to issues such as improving women's lives, increasing critical thinking in adult literacy learners, or improving institutional responses to part-time learners. As part of the project, learners are encouraged to engage in rigorous self-assessment of knowledge, skills, and attitudes learned in the process. They frequently work collaboratively to establish and maintain relationships with others in the program and with their advisors. As a result, they informally acquire skills that they can continue to use when the master's program is completed.

Continuous Construction of Meaning and Knowledge. This master's program encourages practitioners to identify problems and challenges in their own workplaces and to find ways to solve or address them. Learners are asked to complete a learning narrative at the beginning of the master's program, and to submit a comprehensive assessment of their formal, informal, and incidental learning before completing their theses. The learning assessment process challenges learners to reflect critically on their learning intents and to examine ways to improve their practice. The faculty member interacts with the learners and responds in writing to their ideas. By integrating formal and informal learning, this master's program honors professionals' considerable capacity to learn informally in their workplaces.

Engaging in Dialogue. As an informal learning strategy, dialogue is also immensely effective for spiritual growth (English, 1999b). By dialogue I mean the interpersonal connections and interchanges among people that encourage and promote their spiritual development. Current workplace education literature heralds the importance of dialogue. Although this literature has been much maligned for its misappropriation of spirituality to further the cause of the bottom line (Fenwick and Lange, 1998), to its credit it has also advanced the notion of meaningful dialogue as essential to organizational learning (Ellinor and Gerard, 1998; Gerard and Teurfs, 1999; Senge, 1990). The use of dialogue is key in focusing on issues of central importance, assisting in the dissolution of barriers, and promoting collaboration and partnership. Ellinor and Gerard, along with Senge, promote dialogue as an integral component of building an effective organization. Dialogue points to the growing need to recognize the other as an extension of one's self, not as alien or foreign. For adult educators, dialogue holds numerous possibilities for supporting spiritual development.

To illustrate this strategy, I use an example from the health care sector. Elements of this sector have embraced a health promotion approach to community living. Community participation, adult learning principles, and dialogue are important aspects of promoting health. Rather than focusing on the treatment of illness, health educators, especially public health nurses and community nutritionists, are becoming directly involved with community groups. Collectively they are trying to promote healthy lifestyles, and to enable the communities themselves to assess the multiple determinants of their health (for example, economics, social support, and health care services), strategize about solutions to their problems, learn from each other, and become proactive in government and community decisions that affect their present and future health.

An effective example of this approach occurred when community health educators and researchers implemented a health promotion project called People Assessing Their Health (PATH) (1997). By conducting a series of small group sessions in three communities, community facilitators helped participants to assess their health and become more involved in decisions that affected their health. They gathered in settings such as kitchens and community halls. One of the key questions asked was, What makes our community healthy? The dialogue process resulted in a comprehensive report, as well as in the development of three resource tools (health impact assessment tools) for other communities to use in assessing their health. The informal learning strategy of facilitating meaningful dialogue enabled community members to identify the supports and challenges to healthy living, and to use this information to assess the potential health impact of programs and policies on their community. The strengthening of community and the direct engagement of the residents in determining their future is the spiritual basis of the PATH project.

Strong Sense of Self. Consistent with the principles of health promotion, PATH begins with the assumption that individuals know a great deal about health, although they may not know a great deal about the health care system. This project began with people in their own communities. Project facilitators asked them what they thought, what they had experienced, and what they could do to promote health and make decisions about policies that might affect their health. The facilitators honored the learners' stories about health and challenged them to analyze why and how factors such as illiteracy and inadequate educational opportunities affected their health. PATH honored the learners and invited them to share their everyday experiences as valuable contributions to knowledge. PATH honored the development of self through opportunities for dialogue. In Chapter One of this volume, Vella refers to such an approach as a *spirited epistemology.*

Care, Concern, and Outreach to Others. As a health promotion strategy, PATH employed the essentials of good adult learning principles: a participatory approach, extensive dialogue, valuing of community and individual experience, respect for adults as Subjects of their own learning, and attention to problems that learners experience in their everyday lives. Most important, this health promotion strategy of assisting communities to dialogue collectively in order to identify and share knowledge and concerns about health was a way of building relationships, strengthening group identity, and facilitating informal learning. The PATH project acknowledged the need for learning in collaboration with others, and for health educators to reach out to the community and foster healthy practices such as independence, proactive living, and informal learning. The planning of the project itself was participatory in that it was initiated by a local woman's association, a university extension, and public health professionals. One of the major intentions of this project was outreach—specifically to increase mutual understanding, community connections, and information sharing among people in different communities in the region.

Continuous Construction of Meaning and Knowledge. The opportunities for dialogue were numerous in the PATH project. Storytelling among the community participants was identified as a strong and effective tool for facilitating discussion. In some cases, stories about a health-related concern were prepared beforehand and shared in the group, after which participants examined why the incident happened, what they learned from it, and what could be done about it—essentially the learning cycle of Kolb (1984). The facilitation of meaningful dialogue was key in assisting the participants to make sense of their community health experiences, such as being unable to access adequate medical assistance because of cost and distance, and to plan for the future. Through the collective process of creating an image, such as a clock or a tree, each community was able to identify what was happening to them, their communities, and why. Meaning making is intricately connected to the spiritual dimensions of adult learning.

Implications for Practice

Each of the three strategies for informal learning is intricately related to the others. It would be rare for any person to engage in one process without incorporating segments of the others. For instance, dialogue is an essential component of mentoring. Nevertheless, each of the three strategies can be examined separately for suggestions for implementation.

Mentoring can be used to foster spiritual development in many of the same ways that the leaders of the Antigonish Movement utilized it. Adult educators can initiate mentorship structures in their places of practice, and they can encourage individuals to mentor, to pass on their knowledge, skills, and attitudes to mentees and instill in them the social values of the field. They can do as Tompkins did and stand behind the new employees and learners, supporting them and expecting the best from them. Adult educators can have a genuine attitude of welcome for neophytes in the field, appreciating their abilities and fostering in them a shared commitment for the common good. Adult educators can promote the notion of mentorship as a spiritual practice requiring self-discipline, diminishment of ego, and a mutuality of engagement that truly assists the mentor and mentee alike in achieving self-actualization.

To foster a spiritual dimension in self-directed learners, the adult educator can promote relationship building among learners and between learners and educators. Connections can be maintained through listservs, e-mail, fax, and telephone, along with personal contact. By promoting these connections, the educator can help dispel the notion that the self-directed learner must be isolated. They can also foster spiritual development by encouraging engagement in academic projects that have personal meaning and value, projects that help the adult learner make sense of experience and prompt them to improve their practice continuously, even when the program they are taking is completed. By making the learning immediate, personal, and relevant, and by encouraging journal writing, the adult educator can increase the opportunity for learner fulfillment and spiritual development.

Adult educational leaders in organizations as varied as business, health, or religions have numerous possibilities for engendering meaningful dialogue that leads to informal learning. The provision of safe spaces and the encouragement of participation in dialogue can ensure that participants' voices and ideas are honored. Meaningful dialogue can take place only by creating secure places, such as local health promotion assessment groups where participants are coequal and where individuals' ideas are respected. In an organizational context, adult educators might sponsor brown-bag lunches or encourage workers to lead seminars on topics of personal concern, such as health. Adult educators also can engender learning by modeling and initiating constructive dialogue in their own planning and design of educational experiences.

Concluding Comments

The spiritual dimensions of adult learning are indeed complex. They are spiritual in that they are relational, people-centered opportunities for meaningful dialogue, connected to personal and social fulfillment. They are all aspects of an authentic spiritual development process for adult educators. Although all humans have spiritual aspects of their being, not all are aware of this dimension in their lives. Informal and incidental learning provide the context and support that nurture this spiritual component.

The challenge for adult educators is to tap these moments of genuine connection and be aware of them in their own lives and in their practices. In summary, then, I am not only promoting strategies for spiritual development that informal learning can foster, but also encouraging adult educators to learn about their own ways of relating and being in the world—their expressly spiritual dimension.

In that we bring all of ourselves to the teaching and learning act, we are all spiritual beings—a point that Vogel makes in Chapter Two. Those who facilitate informal and incidental learning need to be aware that the spiritual is very much embodied in the teaching and learning process.

References

Brookfield, S. *Adult Learners, Adult Education and the Community.* Buckingham, U.K.: Open University Press, 1983.

Caffarella, R. S. "Self-Directed Learning." In S. B. Merriam (ed.), *An Update on Adult Learning Theory.* New Directions for Adult and Continuing Education, no. 57. San Francisco: Jossey-Bass, 1993.

Candy, P. *Self-Direction for Lifelong Learning: A Comprehensive Guide to Theory and Practice.* San Francisco: Jossey-Bass, 1991.

Daloz, L. *Effective Teaching and Mentoring.* San Francisco: Jossey-Bass, 1986.

Ellinor, L., and Gerard, G. *Dialogue: Rediscover the Transforming Power of Conversation.* New York: Wiley, 1998.

English, L. M. *Mentoring in Religious Education.* Birmingham, Ala.: Religious Education Press, 1998.

English, L. M. "Informal and Incidental Teaching Strategies in Lay-Led Parishes." *Religious Education: An Interfaith Journal of Spirituality, Growth, and Transformation*, 1999a, 94 (3), 300–312.

English, L. M. "Learning from Changes in Religious Leadership." *International Journal of Lifelong Education,* 1999b, *18* (6), forthcoming.

Ervin, E. "Power, Frustration and 'Fierce Negotiation' in Mentoring Relationships: Four Women Tell Their Stories." *Women's Studies,* 1995, *24,* 447–481.

Fenwick, T. J., and Lange, E. "Spirituality in the Workplace: The New Frontier of HRD." *Canadian Journal for the Study of Adult Education,* 1998, *12* (1), 63–87.

Gehrke, N. J. "On Preserving the Essence of Mentoring as One Form of Teacher Leadership." *Journal of Teacher Education,* 1988a, *39* (1), 43–45.

Gehrke, N. J. "Toward a Definition of Mentoring. *Theory into Practice,* 1988b, *27* (3), 190–194.

Gerard, G., and Teurfs, L. "Dialogue and the Organizational Transformation." [http://www.vision-nest.com/cbw/Dialogue.html]. Jan. 1999.

Gillen, M. A. "Spiritual Lessons from the Antigonish Movement." In B. Spencer, S. M. Scott, and A. Thomas (eds.), *Learning for Life: Canadian Readings in Adult Education.* Toronto: Thompson Educational Publishing, 1998.

Kolb, D. A. *Experiential Learning: Experience as the Source of Learning and Development.* Englewood Cliffs, N.J.: Prentice Hall, 1984.

Kram, K. "Phases of the Mentor Relationship." *Academy of Management Journal,* 1983, *26* (4), 608–625.

Levinson, D. *Seasons of a Man's Life.* New York: Knopf, 1978.

Lotz, J., and Welton, M. R. *The Life and Times of Father Jimmy.* Wreck Cove, Nova Scotia: Breton Books, 1997.

MacKeracher, D.M.G. *Making Sense of Adult Learning.* Toronto: Culture Concepts, 1996.

Merriam, S. B., and Heuer, B. "Meaning-Making, Adult Learning and Development: A Model with Implications for Practice." *International Journal of Lifelong Education,* 1996, *15* (4), 243–255.

People Assessing Their Health. *PATHways to Building Healthy Communities in Eastern Nova Scotia: The PATH Project Resource.* Antigonish, Nova Scotia: People Assessing Their Health, 1997.

Schneiders, S. "Theology and Spirituality: Strangers, Rivals or Partners." *Horizons,* 1986, *13* (2), 253–274.

Senge, P. *The Fifth Discipline: The Art and Practice of the Learning Organization.* New York: Doubleday, 1990.

Walker, D. "The Autonomous Person and Self-Directed Learning." In P. Jarvis and N. Walters (eds.), *Adult Education and Theological Interpretations.* Malabar, Fla.: Krieger, 1993.

Watkins, K. E., and Marsick, V. J. "Towards a Theory of Informal and Incidental Learning." *International Journal of Lifelong Education,* 1992, *2* (4), 287–300.

Yeaxlee, B. *Spiritual Values in Adult Education.* 2 vols. London: Oxford University Press, 1925.

Zeldin, M. "Touching the Future: The Promise of Mentoring." In M. Zeldin and S. S. Lee (eds.), *Touching the Future: Mentoring and the Jewish Professional.* Los Angeles: Hebrew Union College—Jewish Institute of Religion, 1995.

LEONA M. ENGLISH is assistant professor of adult education at St. Francis Xavier University in Antigonish, Nova Scotia, Canada.

4

The learning contract has been renamed the learning covenant to emphasize the spiritual dimension of the contract. The learner develops and enters into a written contractual agreement with a facilitator.

The Learning Covenant

R.E.Y. Wickett

Adult educators who facilitate learning often work in relationships that have the potential to encourage spiritual growth and development. The process of learning and the close working relationships that often develop as a result are good examples of what Vella refers to in Chapter One of this volume as a *spirited epistemology*. An epistemology may be spirited regardless of whether the substantive content of the learning is spiritual. For example, an adult literacy educator who views the learning process as a privileged teaching event may not necessarily view the curriculum as spiritual.

Consequently, it is important for persons who work with adult learners on a regular basis to learn to appreciate the rich variety of experiences that learners bring to the learning situation, and the potential for spiritual growth that might come about as a result of their interactions with the learner. More important, adult educators must consider the nature of the relationships that develop as they interact with learners, and the spiritual dimensions of this interaction. One way that this can be done is through the use of the learning covenant, a model rooted in the ancient concept of covenant that has important implications for the relationship between the learner and the adult educator.

This chapter begins with a general overview of covenants, explains the concept of the learning covenant, elaborates on the conditions for establishing covenants such as relationships and on the spiritual dimensions of both learning and covenants, and presents a learning covenant model that can be used in a variety of adult education settings. The essence of learning presented in this educational model and referred to as the learning covenant is its adherence to the need for a high-quality relationship between the learner and the adult educator. The model also provides a vehicle by which learners can be empowered while at the same time engaging in carefully planned, individualized learning activities.

NEW DIRECTIONS FOR ADULT AND CONTINUING EDUCATION, no. 85, Spring 2000   © Jossey-Bass Publishers

Historical Evidence of Covenants

The history of covenants and covenant relationships begins in the very early days of civilization. Our concept of covenants has evolved and expanded over time. While the language or term used may change, the basic concept of an agreement, usually formal, between two or more persons to do or not do something remains the same. Modern agreements such as treaties and contracts are derivatives of the earliest forms of covenants. However, a covenant differs from a contract in that it emphasizes the relationship and not the content of the agreement. This focus distinguishes the covenant from a contract, which emphasizes doing or not doing.

Covenants may be traced back to Mesopotamian society (Paul, 1970). The purpose of covenants, as Paul points out, was to provide a framework for human interaction that would help societies and individuals function in appropriate ways. These early covenants were highly important ways of establishing the rights and responsibilities of both parties. Because early societies believed in some form of higher power or God, the spiritual dimension was necessarily present when people formed covenants and in the living out of the covenant.

The origins of covenants as they are currently known are found in societies that have been influenced by a Judeao-Christian ethos. The Mosaic covenant, for instance, can be interpreted as the governing principles of our current law. The Ten Commandments bound the people of Israel to God and set out clearly their mutual commitments to each other. The earliest concepts of the law drawn from these basic principles are recorded in the Bible.

Since the basic element of covenants is relationship, parties to covenants accept their parts willingly as a way to commit to others and to guarantee a certain result. In an adult learning situation, a learning covenant can facilitate learning and increase self-directedness in learners by establishing responsibilities and deciding on outcomes. It is important to remember the spiritual nature of covenants and the contexts in which earlier covenants were used in order to infuse a spiritual dimension in covenants established today. For this reason, adult educators should examine the conditions of historical covenants that are still relevant today and apply these provisions.

Relationships and Context for Learning

The relationship between the adult educator and the learner is central to the process of interactive learning. Malcolm Knowles (in his book *The Modern Practice of Adult Education*, 1980) and many other adult educators have placed the interactive dimension at the heart of the adult learning experience. If the relationship between educator and learner is important in a learning situation that is not regarded as religious or sacred, it has an even deeper meaning in the context of the relationship that this volume describes as spiritual.

Leon MacKenzie (1982) and John Elias (1993), two adult religious educators, stress the importance of a supportive learning climate and a positive relationship between the learner and the adult educator. Bruce Joyce and Marsha Weil (1986) also describe various models for teaching that provide a framework for planning and implementing face-to-face interactions between teachers and learners. These authors stress the importance of good relationships among learners in groups of any size and between the learner and the educator in any learning activity.

Clearly, the time and energy put into building these relationships on the basic principles of safety, respect, and honor are essential for strengthening the relationships. This type of environment is what Elias (1993) refers to as a healthy interpersonal climate. In fact, most models for teaching and learning have an important interpersonal dimension.

I describe the importance of this interpersonal dimension and the interaction that generally results in my 1991 book *Models of Adult Religious Education Practice,* in which I define a model as a framework that will "assist the educator to understand the nature of the learner's situation and to create a context in which the learner will be enabled to learn and grow through an appropriate process" (p. 3). The focus in my definition is clearly on the learner; the educator is defined in relation to the learner. This definition highlights the educator's need to be interactive with the learner.

The book describes what I refer to as the *learning covenant,* an alternative learning model rooted in the literature of adult education, particularly in Knowles's (1986) learning contract model. In the previous chapter, Leona English describes how a learning contract has been employed in a self-directed master of adult education program. Actually, contracts can be established in a variety of learning settings. For example, they can be established between employers and employees in business and used to promote a learning climate in the workplace and to increase employees' knowledge, skills, and attitudes. In the true spirit of contract, such agreements must be beneficial to both parties.

Covenants are similar to contracts in many ways, but they differ in that covenants include a strong spiritual dimension, especially the capacity to relate, which is innate to humanity. The learning covenant, like a contract, involves establishing learning objectives, naming the strategies to be used for accomplishing these objectives, setting time lines, identifying resources, and outlining criteria for evaluation.

Spiritual Dimensions of Learning

According to Henri Nouwen (1975), the spiritual can be discovered in the three dimensions of human experience: with ourselves, with others, and beyond the human to the source of all spiritual life. In his book *Reaching Out: The Three Movements of the Spiritual Life,* Nouwen describes the human ability to grow spiritually through the recognition of the spiritual dimensions with ourselves, with others, and beyond the human to the source of all spiritual life. In his opinion, it is through the two dimensions of spirituality that exist beyond ourselves that we can truly learn to grow in understanding.

Moving Beyond Ourselves. The ability to move beyond ourselves is key to the success of the covenant relationship and should not be forgotten. It is only within the broader context of these two dimensions—with others and beyond the human—that the relationship with others can make its maximum contribution to our spiritual development.

Growing in Relationship. Nouwen describes the relationship between learner and adult educator as one that involves finding "a hospitable place where life may be lived without fear and where community can be found" (1975, p. 46). This is the space in which relationships can be fully developed and experienced. The term that Nouwen uses to describe the context in which relationships can develop is *hospitality*, which he defines as the creation of "a free and friendly space" in which people can enter to become friends (p. 50). In the second chapter of this volume, Linda Vogel elaborates on the experience of place as helping to ground our spirituality, as a way of connecting the ordinary and the sacred.

Hospitality. The space in which hospitality occurs, to which Nouwen refers, is not a space that requires others to be like us. Rather, it is a space that Nouwen describes as "a friendly emptiness where people can enter and discover themselves as created free." He says, "Hospitality is not an invitation to adopt the lifestyle of the host, but the gift of a chance for the guest to find his own" (1975, p. 51). This task is not easy, because most adult educators have a tendency to control and direct the learning process. To do otherwise requires what Vella refers to in Chapter One as "slaying the dominating professor in myself." This change often requires a psychological shift on the part of adult educators as they relinquish control to learners. Adult educators must learn to trust and also believe in learners' ability and desire to achieve success.

Nouwen stresses the importance of hospitality in relationships between educators and learners and cautions about avoiding the types of relationships in which there is fear because these kinds of relationships are counterproductive to the learning process. Nouwen uses the term *affirming* to describe a positive relationship. He regards affirmation, encouragement, and support as important factors in the learning process. In brief, hospitality is central to an effective covenant, in which learning is involved.

Limitations. Nouwen reminds adult educators that they are not the only ones who have the potential to influence students. Their interactions with each other and with other human resources may be as valuable as or more valuable than their interactions with an educator. In fact, the covenant relationship makes it possible for the adult educator and the learner to engage with each other in a way that is supportive of adult learning. The learning covenant supports the type of relationship that Nouwen believes is desirable for both the learner and the educator, if the spiritual in the three dimensions of human experience is to be realized.

Spiritual Dimensions of Covenants

Because earlier societies viewed the world as having an important spiritual dimension, the presence of a spiritual dimension in covenants was taken for granted. Oaths were sworn to uphold covenants, thereby evoking the spiritual connection to uphold the covenant and bind both parties. In modern society, people generally no longer think in this way, but there are exceptions. Robert Sevensky (1982) and Dennis Kenny (1980) put forward the claim that a higher spiritual power or God has a relationship with the professional who works with clients. Sevensky refers to this relationship in the medical profession, and Kenny makes reference to this kind of relationship within clinical, pastoral fields. These authors urge professionals to consider ways in which the spiritual dimension can be included in their work. When adult educators use learning covenants with their students, they should understand that the very term implies a spiritual dimension, because the emphasis is on the relationship rather than on the content of the agreement.

Part of the difficulty that adult educators encounter today when using learning covenants with their students is misconceptions about the covenant concept and its meaning. Students often confuse the word *covenant* with the word *contract,* which has legal overtones that students often find frightening. In contrast, the covenant approach focuses on the spiritual connection, thereby minimizing the sense of a legal commitment. As we understand them today, covenants have come to our society through a complicated process of change and adaptation.

Conditions of the Covenant

All forms of covenants exist with conditions and within contexts. Each has a reason for existence in the minds of the parties who undertake them. Covenants have been conducted and are conducted currently with certain conditions to ensure effectiveness. The conditions of covenants apply to both parties: a level of commitment, a sense of responsibility, a sense of respect for the other person, benefits, sanctions, connection with other aspects of society and life experience, and an evolving nature (Wickett, 1995, p. 69). Each condition must be considered if maximum benefit is to be derived from the adult learning process. To neglect one condition would put the covenant in jeopardy. Taken together, these conditions provide a recipe for success.

A Level of Commitment. The commitment made to the learning process can not only ensure success in the acquisition of substantive content but it can also reflect the relationship between the parties. For example, an adult literacy educator who in every way possible supports learners who face multiple financial, emotional, and cognitive difficulties as they work toward fulfilling the conditions of a learning covenant is demonstrating commitment. An adult educator's commitment to individuals' personal development, which includes overcoming the various barriers they face, is as important as the educator's commitment to the learning of substantive content. The adult learner must also have a high level of commitment to the learning covenant and be actively involved in all parts of the learning process. The task of the adult educator is take full advantage of the adult learner's commitment.

A Sense of Responsibility. Adult educators must assume a high degree of responsibility for the learning process. This requires that they have special expertise in the subject matter they are teaching in order to ensure the success of the learning process. For example, community college instructors who teach computer courses not only need to be knowledgeable about computers and understand how to teach computer skills, but they must also encourage their students to be Subjects of their learning by helping them set realistic learning goals and identify indicators of success. Adult educators are also responsible for seeing that computer program graduates are competitive in the workplace. The learner, too, should demonstrate a strong sense of responsibility to participate and maximize learning. This mutual sense of responsibility will inevitably draw both parties into a relationship in which the spiritual dimension is recognized and enhanced because it is based on dialogue, respect, and accountability.

A Sense of Respect for the Other Person. Jeffrey Orr and Linda Vogel point out in Chapters Six and Two, respectively, of this volume that respect is central to a spiritually based relationship. The word *respect* refers to the condition of being esteemed or honored, a sense of the worth or excellence of a person. In a learning covenant, adult educators and learners must respect one another as persons and acknowledge the skills and knowledge that each has to offer. For example, nutrition educators who work with senior citizens and help them from time to time to establish goals for changing lifestyle behaviors need to be respectful of the seniors' lifelong experiences as well as of their rights and freedoms. This kind of personal respect provides a basis for interaction and mutual benefit.

Benefits. Learners who have had a successful learning experience often feel overjoyed and proud of their accomplishments. Their self-esteem improves and their desire to continue learning grows and develops. These are the positive benefits of success. Not surprisingly, adult educators who practice a spirited epistemology experience benefits as well. In Chapter Two, Vogel explains that they recognize that "by entering into a 'spirited epistemology' . . . horizons are expanded and all are invited to share in the benefits of that work." This positive feeling is related in part to the quality of the relationship that the educator has had with the learner. It is here that the spiritual dimension is most likely to be evident.

Sanctions. It is impossible to discuss benefits without referring to the sanctions that are a consequence of an unsuccessful learning experience.

Sanctions can best be described as the lack of success. When the adult learner is unsuccessful in acquiring new knowledge or skills, not only has the learner failed, but the adult educator has failed as well. A good example is well-intentioned parents who sign up for a parenting skills course but in spite of their efforts are unsuccessful in changing their relationships with difficult children. Although it is hard to recognize the spiritual dimension in the context of failure, it may well be there in terms of the support and safety of the learning relationship that is required at the time. In the case of the parents, they might have learned to deal with their problem better than they did before, to practice patience, and to find ways of dialoguing with their children.

A Connection with Other Aspects of Society and Life Experience. Learning is connected with a person's everyday life and the community in which the person lives. Unionized workers who are sent on training programs of short duration are in particular need of learning objectives and content that are applicable to their work situations. To view the learning experience in isolation from everyday experience is to miss some valuable aspects of the learning process. The spiritual dimension is best seen through an understanding of the whole person in a social context.

Evolving Nature. As conditions change and as the learner proceeds through the learning process, covenants are bound to change. It is important that the learner and the covenant not be seen as static. For instance, as the adult educator sees the learner develop during the learning process, adaptations can and should be made in order to continue creating space for the learner to grow. A challenge that adult educators often face in this regard is convincing adult learners to be more flexible.

The Learning Covenant Model

The learning process is clearly dynamic, with both parties sharing in the changes that occur. The learning covenant model (Wickett, 1991, 1993, 1999) provides the best illustration of the kind of relationship that can exist between the adult learner and the educator—a relationship that has a spiritual dimension. This model has clear role definitions for both parties. The strength of the learning covenant model is in part found in the fact that it has been used extensively under the guise of a learning contract by various groups, including such professions as nurses and medical doctors, and the business community.

The learning covenant model regards adults as responsible people. In other words, adults who engage in a learning covenant have direct responsibility for many decisions that must be made. They are Subjects of their own learning. Their responsibilities include the planning, conduct, and evaluation of the learning.

The task of adult educators who participate in learning covenants is to facilitate the learner's growth and change by providing a central source of support for the learning process similar to Nouwen's (1975) hospitality. To be successful in carrying out this task, the adult educator must develop an understanding of the learner and of the growth that is occurring.

Relationship. An important dimension of the learning covenant model is the building of a relationship between the educator and the learner. Knowles (1975, 1986), O'Donnell and Caffarella (1990), and Wickett (1991, 1999) all agree on this point. A review of the methodology of learning covenants is particularly valuable when the learner is new to the model. This can be done during an orientation period, during which the tasks involved in the learning covenant are outlined and explained in detail, readings about the covenant process are suggested, examples of covenants are shared with the learners, and opportunities to work on a covenant draft, including feedback on the proposal, are provided. One key feature at the drafting stage of the learning covenant is the identification of the resources that will be required. The finalization of the covenant should occur only after an appropriate process of refinement has been completed. It is at this stage that I stress with my students the importance of clarity, appropriateness, and workability. Dates for meetings and final feedback should be determined at this point.

This period of working together helps the learner to gain confidence in the model. It also provides the adult educator and learner with an opportunity to develop a closer working relationship. One way that these relationships can be developed is through the process of mentoring. An extensive discussion of mentoring as a form of informal learning can be found in Chapter Three, by Leona English.

Content of the Learning. One important step in putting together a learning contract is exploration of the substantive content to be learned. Content is the subjects, or topics, of a book or course. Very often the content is determined by learners' felt need to learn in order to function better in everyday life. Very often this need is determined by where people find themselves in the life cycle. Even in the same program, the reasons that adult learners participate can be very different. An older adult learner might take a course for purely social reasons or out of a desire to learn something new, while a younger person may take the course to advance at work. This variation in reasons for learning often involves complex negotiations between the educator and the learners, so that in the end everyone is reasonably satisfied. The process brings the parties into a close working relationship.

Forming the Covenant. It is during the process of negotiating and conducting the covenant that the adult educator is able to create space for the learner. The learner assumes responsibility for the activities, and the educator, sometimes referred to as the facilitator, guides and supports the learning.

Concluding Thoughts

Covenants have a strong connection with the spiritual dimension, both historically and at the present time. In fact, covenants by their very nature embody a spiritual connection. They incorporate the spiritual dimension of both parties and the spiritual dimension that goes beyond the parties involved in the learning.

Relationships are central to adult learning. Adult educators need to create space for the learner that fosters learning and spiritual growth. Adults who enter learning convents may decide that they need several days to mull over their learning intents, in light of their own spiritual journey. The concept of a hospitable space in which this growth can occur is a challenge that adult educators must face as they respect the learner's ability to grow and change in a manner that is most appropriate for the learner.

References

Elias, J. L. *The Foundations and Practice of Adult Religious Education.* (Rev. ed.) Malabar, Fla.: Krieger, 1993.

Joyce, B., and Weil, M. *Models of Teaching.* Englewood Cliffs, N.J.: Prentice Hall, 1986.

Kenny, D. K. "Clinical Pastoral Education: Making Covenants with God." *The Journal of Pastoral Care,* 1980, *34,* 109–113.

Knowles, M. S. *Self-Directed Learning: A Guide for Learners and Teachers.* Englewood Cliffs, N.J.: Prentice Hall, 1975.

Knowles, M. S. *The Modern Practice of Adult Education: From Pedagogy to Andragogy.* River Grove, Ill.: Follett, 1980.

Knowles, M. S. *Using Learning Contracts.* San Francisco: Jossey-Bass, 1986.

MacKenzie, L. *The Religious Education of Adults.* Birmingham, Ala.: Religious Education Press, 1982.

Nouwen, H.J.M. *Reaching Out: The Three Movements of the Spiritual Life.* New York: Doubleday, 1975.

O'Donnell, J. M., and Caffarella, R. S. "Learning Contracts." In M. W. Galbraith (ed.), *Adult Learning Methods: A Guide for Effective Instruction.* Malabar, Fla.: Krieger, 1990.

Paul, S. "Studies in the Book of the Covenant in the Light of Cuneiform and Biblical Law." Supplements to *Vitus Testamentum.* Leiden, the Netherlands: E. J. Brill, 1970.

Sevensky, R. L. "The Religious Physician." *Journal of Religion and Health,* 1982, *21,* 254–263.

Wickett, R.E.Y. *Models of Adult Religious Education Practice.* Birmingham, Ala.: Religious Education Press, 1991.

Wickett, R.E.Y. "Contract Learning and the Covenant." In P. Jarvis and N. Walters (eds.), *Adult Education and Theological Interpretations.* Malabar, Fla.: Krieger, 1993.

Wickett, R.E.Y. "Teaching and Learning in the Context of the Biblical Covenant." *Panorama: International Journal of Comparative Religious Education and Values,* 1995, *7,* 65–71.

Wickett, R.E.Y. *How to Use the Learning Covenant in Religious Education: Working with Adults.* Birmingham, Ala.: Religious Education Press, 1999.

R.E.Y. WICKETT is professor in the Department of Educational Foundations, College of Education, University of Saskatchewan, Saskatoon, Canada.

5

Parish nursing education is an example of continuing professional education that intentionally addresses the spiritual dimension of learning as it relates to the adult learner, both personally and professionally. The continuing professional education course described here is based on a spirited epistemology, a learner-centered approach.

Continuing Professional Education: A Spiritually Based Program

Lynda W. Miller

Continuing professional education (CPE) is the education of professionals after their initial preservice training and induction or licensing into professional practice (Cervero, 1992). Many professions today require their members to undertake CPE in order to maintain and enhance their professional practice. A good example is the health care professions. One problem with many CPE offerings is an exclusive focus on technical expertise without regard to other types of learning, such as emotional, relational, intuitive, and spiritual. Another problem is that the participant is often viewed as a passive recipient rather than as an active participant in the creation of knowledge. Individuals are often limited in what they can learn when the learning is separated from who they are as individuals and as professionals.

This chapter provides an example of a CPE course that is designed to prepare professional registered nurses (RNs) for the emerging specialty practice of parish nursing. To set the stage for discussing this program, I first define the term *parish nursing,* describe its contexts, and explain the parish nurse's role. In the following sections I describe the Miller Model©, explain the course I developed based on this model, and present some evaluation findings about the course.

What Is Parish Nursing?

I have defined Christian *parish nursing* as "a health promotion ministry, preventative in focus, in which faith and health are clearly linked, and spiritual care is central" (Miller, 1996a, p. 11). Its broader designation, *congregational health ministries,* expresses a deliberate attempt on the part of Christianity to reclaim its historical role of promoting health and the healing of body and soul. I view parish nursing as both something old and something new. The term and its current definition are new, but its foundations are old and can be traced back to the beginning of Christianity.

The Contexts of Parish Nursing

The rapid growth of parish nursing education programs across North America in the past few years is a reflection of what has been happening in at least four contexts: our society in general, the health care system, the nursing profession, and faith communities.

Societal Context. Today there is a growing interest in the body-mind-spirit connection and holistic health care. Popular magazines report poll findings: baby boomers "say they are 'spiritual'" is one of a number of signs of "renewed interest in the sacred," even a "great awakening," among ordinary people affirming religious faiths or embarking on complex spiritual searches (Emberley, 1998/1999, p. 101).

Health Care System. In recent years there has been a conscious shifting of focus in our health care system from the high-tech tertiary care in hospitals to primary care and preventive services in the community (Martin, 1996). Despite health care reforms, there is still a gap between supply and demand. The increasing frustrations and burnout of nurses result from the gap between the current realities of the system and the ideal of whole-person care that professional nurses want to provide.

Professional Education. Continuing education is paramount in all professions to address practitioners' need to update their knowledge and skills (Houle, 1980). This need is particularly strong among professional nurses, given the realities and complexities of their diverse practice settings and the implications of codes of ethics and the regulatory standards of licensing bodies. For decades nursing educators have not adequately addressed the spiritual dimension of their practice, and today a desire is being expressed, particularly by Christian nurses, to reclaim the profession's spiritual roots, especially the caring aspect (Miller, 1997).

Faith Communities. Holistic approaches to human experience may be found both in various long-established religious traditions and in more recent expressions associated with New Age philosophies. Parish nursing is an example of a holistic approach to health care that is deeply rooted within, and specifically defined by, the Christian faith community. The promotion of health in the Christian churches through designated members can be traced to the Church's earliest history; hence some view the emergence of parish nursing as the nursing profession's need to reclaim its role of caring for people in both soul and body (Zersen, 1994). Although the focus in this chapter is on nurses in the Christian faith community, the literature reports a growing interest in spirituality among nurses of various religious and spiritual perspectives (Weaver and others, 1998).

Today, moreover, health care and health promotion are no longer viewed as the domains of health professionals only. Besides the emergence of parish nursing programs, lay health ministries such as pastoral and palliative care are also multiplying. These various innovative and collaborative endeavors are providing opportunities for both health care institutions and faith communities to reconnect in practical, empowering ways that benefit both the people served and the partnering institutions.

The Role of the Parish Nurse

Today, parish nurses work in collaboration with clergy, lay ministry workers, professionals, and others, both within a local congregation and in public and private sector organizations in the wider community. Parish nurses provide a wide range of services such as medical screenings, healthy lifestyle programs, individual health counseling, visiting the sick, support groups, and linkages with health-related community resources and services. What distinguishes parish nursing from other kinds of nursing practice is its integration of faith and health. I picture the parish nurse as standing with one foot in the health care system and the other foot in the faith community, and speaking two languages—"medicalese" and "churchese." The role is professionally autonomous and takes place in a communal context. It requires high-level competencies and maturity in the Christian faith—hence the need for spiritually based CPE.

A Model for Parish Nursing

Since Westberg's (1990) initial project in 1985 with six parish nurses in Chicago, there has been rapid expansion of practical and educational programs in the United States, involving an estimated six thousand nurses in the United States alone. Interest has been growing steadily in Canada since 1995 (Martin, 1996). The development of a theoretical base for parish nursing, however, has not kept pace (Miller, 1996a). For example, in 1995 I discovered, while reviewing the literature in the area of general nursing theory, that there was a paucity of literature on the spiritual dimensions of nursing practice. However, in the area of mental health nursing, an interest in the spiritual and religious variables of practice was growing (Weaver and others, 1998). I failed to find a conceptual framework that was particularly associated with parish nursing. Based on these findings I decided, during my doctoral studies, to develop a conceptual model for parish nursing now known as The Miller Model© (Miller, 1996a).

This model is described fully in other publications (Miller, 1996a, 1996b, 1997). In this chapter, I provide a brief explanation. Like other theoretical frameworks in the nursing literature, this model addresses basic concepts of nursing, health, personhood, and community. What distinguishes the model is its central focus on the spiritual. Developed from an explicitly biblical Christian worldview, it is faith centered and Christ centered (Miller 1996a).

By definition, nursing conceptual models like the Miller Model are intentionally abstract. To be made more useful they have to be translated into more specific or practical terms. This is what I did when I used the model as the framework for the parish nursing course.

I have divided the course into five modules that reflect the major components of the Miller Model (see Figure 5.1). Because there are not yet any textbooks on parish nursing, I put together a course manual that contains twenty-nine reprints of articles from current publications along with my informal notes on the topics. These notes serve as a guide for the students

Figure 5.1. Components and Major Concepts of the Miller Model©

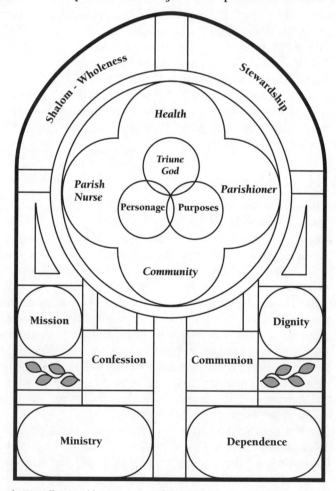

©1996 Lynda W. Miller. Used by permission of the author.

as they read the articles. In addition to the required readings, the appendixes include lists of optional references, resource materials, and sources of further information and support.

Spiritual Focus of the Course. The course has an obvious spiritual dimension, in both its content and its methodology. Students also expect, when they sign up for the course, to have their spiritual life experience and knowledge validated and enhanced.

Course Content. Even though the course is on parish nursing, the emphasis is on what nurses can and must do as spiritual caregivers. Most nurses who take the course are already experienced in nursing. Therefore the objective of the course is not to teach nursing terms or concepts but rather to explore and examine the spiritual resources that nurses can use while caring for patients. This is an area that is underrepresented in nursing literature and curricula. Karen Soeken (1989), a nurse researcher, points out that there is "little published research in this area to address, for example, whether spiritual care should be a part of nursing, the signs and symptoms of spiritual diagnoses, how the spiritual needs of clients can be assessed most effectively, or how spiritual interventions differ from emotional support" (p. 356). Even within the literature, there is no consensus on the meaning of *spiritual care* or *spirituality*.

I have attempted to address this problem by grounding the course in the Christian worldview represented in the Miller Model, which sees the person as an "inspirited whole"; health as biblical shalom-wholeness; parish nursing as a Christian calling to provide competent, compassionate care as a coparticipant; and the parish as both the church and the wider community. Figure 5.2 represents this view of the human spirit as that which animates and integrates all of the complex and interrelated aspects of the person. Of the six aspects (spiritual, physical, mental, emotional, social, and cultural), the spiritual is central. The figure also illustrates some health-promoting resources that surround the person.

The resources are of two kinds: personal and interpersonal. The personal resources are family, God, faith community, and friends. The interpersonal are health care services, social services, vocation, and recreation. I also suggest that students try to imagine a hand in which the fingers and thumb each represent the physical, mental, emotional, social, and cultural aspects of the person, and the palm of the hand represents the spiritual.

Course Methodology. The course is taught by the following means: use of a course manual; correspondence with the instructor (course facilitator) by e-mail, fax, and toll-free telephone for four hours per week; use of instructional and reflective activities; and through three assignments to which extensive written feedback is provided. The course manual is written in a conversational format, inviting students to engage on a spiritual level. I pose rhetorical questions, provide biblical texts on which to meditate, and share information about my own faith background and spiritual journey. For example, in discussing the role of the parish nurse as an "integrator of faith and

Figure 5.2. Aspects of the Whole Person and Health-Promoting
Resources: The Miller Model©

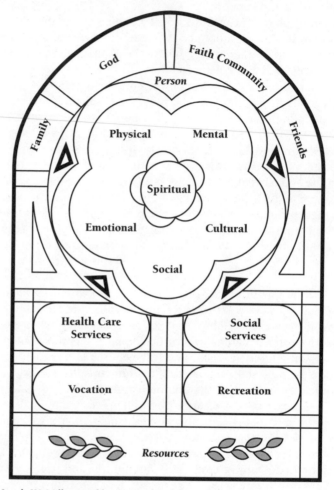

health," I raise the questions I asked myself as a student when pondering the
same phrase. This approach is in keeping with Vogel's idea in Chapter Two
of reckoning with the spiritual lives of adult educators.

As part of the instructional activities, I explain why particular readings
have been selected, help identify key points, and point out the underlying
worldviews. Students use workbooks with blank spaces in which to make
notes and write questions for discussion with me or others later.

In recognition of the significant role of critical reflection in adult learning, and of the need for these students to do theological reflection, I have

included specific reflective activities in each module. These are also presented in workbook style, including blank spaces for creative drawing. The spiritual dimension is the focus of most of these reflections. Following are some samples (Miller, 1998, pp. 33–34):

Sample 1: Take a few minutes now to ponder Westberg's (1990) descriptive phrase, "integrator of faith and health." Following are some questions to ask yourself:

- How do you integrate your personal faith and your personal health?
- What personal life experiences come to mind?
- Was there an instance when your own health was challenged?
- What faith beliefs and practices were involved in that experience?
- How do you integrate faith and health in your work as a professional nurse?
- What work experiences come to mind?
- What faith beliefs and practices were involved in that experience?
- What or who influenced you in these experiences?

Sample 2: Having considered biblical examples, reflect now for a moment on your own personal calling and respond to these questions:

- Can you remember when you first became aware that God was calling you to change direction and to dedicate yourself to others in a deliberate way?
- Did you sacrifice anything to respond to God's call?
- How is God calling you today—that is, which persons, communities, or events in your life continue to make you conscious of God's call?
- What do you think that call is asking of you?
- In what ways does parish nursing relate to that calling?

Of the three course assignments, two involve reflective activities and specific tools for assessing spiritual health. The first assignment requires students to complete an inventory of their attitudes, values, knowledge, and skills, both personal and professional. This includes using a values survey (Miller, 1998, pp. vi-vii) and two self-assessment tools that focus on "spiritual health" and "spiritual talents." The second assignment requires students to assess the health of someone in their local faith community. They may select any one tool or a combination of tools or approaches from their course readings to use to evaluate all aspects of the person (physical, mental, emotional, social, cultural, and spiritual) in addition to the person's health concerns and health resources. Students are also asked to evaluate critically the spiritual assessment tools and questions they used.

Evaluation of the Course. Students' evaluation of the course, especially of the spiritual dimension, is elicited in a number of ways: through verbal and written conversations with the instructor-facilitator, through a student information survey form, through the formal end-of-course evaluation form requested by the educational institutions offering the course, and through unsolicited statements that appear on the students' assignments.

On the whole, the course evaluations have been positive. Students claim that the course contributed to their spiritual growth and offered a new perspective on nursing. Even students who took the course out of personal interest felt the knowledge they gained could be applied to nursing practice in other settings. For example, when an operating room nurse revised a case assessment tool, she used what she had learned during the course and added a section on spiritual care. Another nurse added a section on spirituality to her in-service training course.

In adult education, application of learning, or what is referred to in the literature as *transfer of learning* (Caffarella, 1994), is viewed as very important. In my own teaching of experienced RNs, I have noted that they expect their courses to have both personal and professional relevance and practicality. Several students have expressed a desire to learn more about the spiritual dimensions of their profession and have suggested that courses on spiritual counseling and spiritual support for nurses be developed.

From the feedback I have received I have learned how the parish nursing course has affected the spiritual life of participants. For example, one student, in her critique of the second assignment, noted, "This was a new experience for me . . . having to ask 'private' questions about spirituality and religion . . . [but] all went well . . . [and the interviewee] and I connected on a fundamental level." Another student made a similar statement after completing her self-inventory assignment: "As I continue with this course of study, it is my goal to prayerfully seek God's leading in my life and allow the course material and assignments to be an avenue of personal growth in my faith journey." Further evidence of spiritual impact is found in this excerpt from a student's e-mail correspondence with me:

> I do think that clients will be surprised when nurses ask them about their spiritual health. I see a risk here as well. If a person has never thought about his or her spiritual health, but is asked about it by a nurse, and starts thinking about things that he or she would rather not think about, are we then doing the patient more harm than good? In doing some of the reflective exercises, I have found myself getting deep in thought about some things I have never thought about before, and asking myself a lot of questions that I don't have answers for yet. I did not anticipate this when I started this course!

Conclusion

In concluding this chapter, I must admit that I too have done some deep thinking as I have developed and facilitated the parish nursing course. I too have questions yet to be answered. But the evidence is clear. The emerging practice of parish nursing is filling a need in the nursing profession. It also challenges other professions to respond in a proactive way to the growing interest in the spiritual dimension of human existence.

References

Caffarella, R. S. *Planning Programs for Adult Learners.* San Francisco: Jossey-Bass, 1994.
Cervero, R. M. "Professional Practice, Learning, and Continuing Education: An Integrated Perspective." *International Journal of Lifelong Education,* 1992, *11* (2), 91–101.
Emberley, P. C. "Searching for Purpose." *Maclean's,* Dec. 28, 1998/Jan. 4, 1999, pp. 100–105.
Houle, C. O. *Continuing Learning in the Professions.* San Francisco: Jossey-Bass, 1980.
Martin, L. B. "Parish Nursing: Keeping Body and Soul Together." *Canadian Nurse,* 1996, *92* (1), 25–28.
Miller, L. W. "A Nursing Conceptual Model Grounded in Christian Faith." Ph.D. dissertation, University of Victoria, British Columbia, 1996a.
Miller, L. W. "Nursing Conceptual Models (and Muddles!)." Paper presented at the Tenth Annual Granger Westberg Symposium on Parish Nursing, Itasca, Ill., Sept. 25–27, 1996b.
Miller, L. W. "Nursing Through the Lens of Faith: A Conceptual Model." *Journal of Christian Nursing,* 1997, *14* (1), 17–21.
Miller, L. W. *Nursing 485: Parish Nursing Course Manual.* Antigonish, Nova Scotia: St. Francis Xavier University, 1998.
Soeken, K. L. "Perspectives on Research in the Spiritual Dimension of Nursing Care." In V. B. Carson (ed.), *Spiritual Dimensions of Nursing Practice.* Philadelphia: Saunders, 1989.
Weaver, A. J., Flannelly, L. T., Flannelly, K. J., Koenig, H. G., and Larson, D. B. "An Analysis of Research on Religious and Spiritual Variables in Three Major Mental Health Nursing Journals, 1991–1995." *Issues in Mental Health Nursing,* 1998, *19* (3), 263–276.
Westberg, G. E., and McNamara, J. W. *The Parish Nurse.* (2nd ed.). Minneapolis: Augsburg Fortress, 1990.
Zersen, D. "Parish Nursing: Twentieth-Century Fad?" *Journal of Christian Nursing,* 1994, *11* (2), 19–21, 45.

LYNDA W. MILLER is principal of Congregational Health Services, Victoria, British Columbia, Canada, and adjunct professor at Concordia University College of Alberta and St. Francis Xavier University, Antigonish, Nova Scotia. She is also commissioned as the parish nurse of her local church (Brentwood Bay, British Columbia) and chairs the Parish Nursing Task Force of the Anglican Diocese of British Columbia.

6

Adult educators have much to learn from Native peoples' focus on the four directions of the medicine wheel: the emotional, physical, spiritual, and cognitive.

Learning from Native Adult Education

Jeffrey A. Orr

As Mary Jane, a Cree elder, passed the eagle feather around the circle, an amazing calm came over my students. For weeks they had been wired increasingly tighter by the institutional pressures of assignment deadlines plus family and work responsibilities, but in the context of the talking circle their tensions and anxieties dissipated. The talking circle, like many Native educational processes, creates a spiritual space for learning by providing people with room to explore issues of great significance to them. The spiritual focus that many Native people bring to adult education is not only a method; it is also a way of being (Graveline, 1998). It is a good example of what Vella, in the first chapter of this volume, refers to as a *spirited epistemology.*

Although spirituality has always occupied a special place in the hearts of Native people, only recently has it been a central organizing feature of Native adult education programs. Native adult educators are more likely today to focus on cultural practices that foster a Native identity that is spiritually rooted (Battiste, 1995; Haig-Brown, 1995; Hampton, 1995; National Indian Brotherhood, 1972).

Education for Native identity centers on cultivating a deepened sense of Native spirituality and culture by focusing on indigenous knowledge (Battiste, 1998; Haig-Brown, 1995; National Indian Brotherhood, 1972). Native adult education programs that reintroduce, preserve, or enhance Native spirituality rather than reproducing mainstream education cultivate an indigenous form of knowledge (Battiste, 1998; Friesen and Orr, 1995; Haig-Brown, 1995; Regnier, 1995; Ross, 1996). Adult educators who are struggling to find fresh possibilities for a more integrated worldview in their practice can learn much from Native adult educators.

This chapter describes how a focus on the spiritual dimensions of Native adult education, as lived through the teachings of the medicine wheel, can enhance Native identity (Hampton, 1995). It draws on published accounts as well as on unpublished research (recorded in my field notes of 1998) that I have conducted with Native adult educators in places where I have worked and continue to work. I recount stories told to me by Native adult educators that focus on ecological and physical teachings, relational teachings, and the teachings of the elders. The stories of Patricia, Matthias, Rose, and Susan point out how spirituality, the fourth direction of the medicine wheel, is manifested in the practices of Native adult educators, and how it can be used to inform Native and non-Native adult education.

Using the Medicine Wheel

The medicine wheel is often referred to as the circle of life. It is an ancient symbol that can be used to express many relationships that involve sets of four, for example, the four cardinal directions—north, south, east, and west; four physical elements of the world—fire, earth, air, water; or the four aspects of nature—mental, spiritual, emotional, and physical. The circle has no beginning or no end. When one sits in a circle, no one is ahead or behind; everyone is together.

The medicine wheel has empowered communities and Native organizations to reorganize, reframe, and recover a self-determining approach to Native adult education (Calliou, 1995; Graveline, 1998; Hampton, 1995). It provides a format for teaching that establishes harmony between physicality, relationality, wisdom of the elders, and spirituality (Calliou, 1995; Graveline, 1998; Hart, 1996; Hart and Holton, 1993; Ross, 1996) and achieves healing and conflict resolution (Calliou, 1995). The medicine wheel is a traditional indigenous way of viewing the world that is both ancient and global (Graveline, 1998). Patricia, a Mi'Kmaq adult educator told me, "When I first saw the medicine wheel I thought it was a western [prairie] thing. . . . As I learned about it I found out that it was holistic. I realized that it was something that we had always done" (Orr, field notes). As Hill (1995) points out, the medicine wheel places the spirit at the center of the knowledge process and seeks balance between its four dimensions rather than privileging any one form of knowing—an insight important for all areas of adult education.

Respect for the spiritual relationships that exist between all things is at the core of the medicine wheel teachings. This is the respect that Vella describes in Chapter One of this volume. The medicine wheel provides a framework for teaching Native values in order to keep spirituality at the center of Native identity. This balance can help to redress the failings of the past and allow people to live differently in the present and future.

Native adult education centers in urban areas typically attract Native people of vastly different cultures, languages, and identities. These centers are turning to the medicine wheel as a way to help Native people live amid this diversity. The spiritual emphasis in such centers tends to acknowledge and promote a universal Native worldview that is referred to as *Pan-Indianism*

(Haig-Brown, 1995). In such contexts, if adult educators are insensitive to the particularities of diverse Native communities, the medicine wheel can become a barrier and may silence the unique cultural perspectives of Native communities. To avoid such a consequence, adult educators must strive to support the linguistic and cultural differences through which spirituality and culture are embodied (Hart, 1996; Francis, 1999; Powers, 1986).

The Medicine Wheel in Adult Education Practice

An andragogy that embraces the balanced approach of all the dimensions of the medicine wheel or sacred circle (Calliou, 1995; Graveline, 1998; Regnier, 1995) is a way to foster a spiritual identity. In the following sections I describe how various Native adult educators have used the medicine wheel in their practices.

An Ecological Spirituality. Matthias, a Cree adult educator who works in a central office in a Native-controlled school system in northern Saskatchewan, told me how his commitment to place and to an ecological worldview has shaped his practice (Friesen and Orr, 1995). Matthias learned an ecological way of being as a child during his time on the land, where he observed his grandparents' respect for Mother Earth. "I watched as my grandfather picked medicinal herbs, for he would always put something back in their place; I learned to be connected to the land," he explained to me. Similarly, Patricia noted, "Spirituality is all around us. We're all in this earth" (Orr, field notes).

The respect for the ecological that we hear in Matthias's and Patricia's stories is common among a wide range of aboriginal nations (Hampton, 1995; Mander, 1991, Miller, 1991; O'Meara and West, 1996). A fundamental view of Mother Earth as a sacred living thing is important to Canadian tribal cultures such as the Plains Cree, Stony, Woodlands Cree, and Mi'Kmaq (Snow, 1977; Ermine, 1995; Friesen and Orr, 1995; Orr, 1998). This way of being is expressed not only by valuing a sense of place and a view of the earth as a living thing, but also by a commitment to holistic patterns of relationships. Vogel has developed this theme of holistic relationships more fully in Chapter Two of this volume.

Native education that focuses on the sacredness of all things in the physical world provides a way of being that responds in a positive way to the destructiveness of modern society (Slattery, 1995) and allows for an ecological consciousness that is centered on how we live on and use the earth. Graveline (1998) stresses the importance of the physical self in relation to the earth as a way to be more connected and balanced. Native adult education that attends to the ecological cultivates harmony between people and all living things. This Native ecological worldview is in tension with many of the adult training programs that have as their objective preparing Native people to work in mining industries that exploit the earth (Saskatchewan Department of Education, 1989) and that are based on capitalist economics. It also counters the dominant perspectives of science, because it sees all the world, including the rocks and clouds, as alive (Mander, 1991). Adult educators who follow this path can help their students examine how aboriginal values have been replaced with Eurocentric values that have contributed to severe ecological consequences resulting from our "massive rearrangement of the North American landscape" (Orr, 1992, p. 130).

Calliou (1995) talks of embodying this sense of the ecological in the physical space of the circle. "In the circle, no individual being (two legged, four legged, mineral, plant, etc.) is deemed 'more than' or 'less than' another, so that treatment which elevates or denigrates one or the other is ruled out" (p. 67). The ecological dimension of spirituality is expressed through holistic forms of andragogy that honor indigenous respect for the circle as a way of organizing teachings. An andragogical practice that draws on the power of the circle allows for an equalization of voices that promotes a shared ownership of knowledge and a collective responsibility for learning. "We use the circle because it is never ending," Patricia told me. "It shows us that we are all equal, there are no corners, it goes round and round" (Orr, field notes).

The Spirituality of Relationships: Teaching Through Sharing and Respect. Rose, a Cree adult educator, who teaches the Cree language to adults, noted that "the gift of giving is one thing that the elders taught me. . . . Whatever the Creator put on Earth was not for you to take and keep, you pass it on at some point" (Friesen and Orr, 1995, p. 30). The indigenous values of sharing and respect are embedded in Rose's Cree language. She passes these values on to others through storytelling because "there are lots of values in these stories" (p. 33). The spiritual dimension of Native languages has been emphasized as a key reason why Native linguists from a variety of language groups preserve Aboriginal languages (Francis, 1999; Powers, 1986).

Storytelling is a process that many Native adult educators use as a way to live spirituality through relationships. Patricia uses story circles to ensure that learners have the opportunity to cultivate collectively their thinking as spiritual beings (Orr, field notes). From her perspective, story circles provide learners with "freedom, and there are no consequences for what they say, as what is said stays in the circle." This relational approach fosters a commitment to their families because it values their family relationships and serves as a way to cultivate the learners' identities.

Susan, a Mi'Kmaq educator, also sees her work at an adult high school as closely connected to relationship building (Orr, 1998). She focuses on relationships through her emphasis on valuing the community in her classroom. Commenting on her own practice, she says, "It's all a community thing in my classroom. The objective is being there and helping one another by supporting one another" (p. 12).

A relational focus directs attention to values that honor the sacredness of the interpersonal. For Native traditionalists, the key values that shape a relational-emotional stance are caring, sharing, honesty, and respect (Calliou, 1995; Graveline, 1998; Orr and Friesen, 1999). Sioui (1992) tells us that all Native peoples of the Americas are united by the way they live out the values of "unity and dignity of all beings" (p. 23).

Rose, Patricia, Matthias, and Susan all live what Ross (1996) calls a relational practice that reinforces community and family dimensions of learning by establishing interconnections with the major players in people's lives. Focusing adult learners' emotional energies on family and friends strengthens their commitment to the indigenous value of the individual as caring for and supporting the life of the group (Hampton, 1995).

Wisdom: Living Spirituality Through Stories of the Elders. The wisdom of the elders is central to understanding and living Native spirituality, because elders hold much of the wisdom that defines traditional Native values. Native adult education must build on this wisdom if it is to reflect these spiritual values accurately. Native adult education practices that honor the wisdom inherent in Native languages and values provide a direction that allows Native people to center themselves in the past so they can embrace the present and the future in a culturally appropriate way. Native wisdom, or knowledge of what is true and right, coupled with good judgment, comes from reflecting on the values that are passed on through the stories of the elders.

Rose has come to know the importance of the wisdom of elders in her work teaching the Cree language to adults (Friesen and Orr, 1995). She sees herself as a bridge between the knowledge of the elders and the more mainstream knowledge of the dominant society. Rose says, "I see myself as a voice in the classroom for elders. As a teacher I am speaking both for elders and for education. . . . You learn to balance the two things. So you just put it into one container" (p. 31). Her role as an adult educator is to keep alive the values that are dying as the elders die. Adult education that embraces the wisdom of the elders helps adult educators focus their teaching on values that emerge from traditional ways such as generosity and respect.

Strategies for Including Native Spirituality in Adult Education

A spiritual way of being in Native adult education requires one to develop harmony not only within oneself but also within relationships with others and the environment, in order to be whole (Graveline, 1998). As Patricia told me, "Once we can feel good about our own inner circle, then the circle escalates. Then we can reach out of the circle if we need help" (Orr, field notes). Harmony means that all four directions must be attended to in equal fashion, with the spirit infusing a person's entire being within the world.

Attending to the Physical Environment. The physical-ecological direction can be introduced in the adult education classroom by centering on the power of the circle. In this way, spirituality can be experienced continuously as part of the interconnectedness of the individual, community, and nature. As Graveline (1998) reminds us, all participants are equal in the circle, and that the process of inviting people to form a "cohesive circle is an integral part of re-establishing interconnectedness" (p. 131). Sharing circles are the vehicle whereby the spiritual dimensions of Native adult education surface as Native people journey toward self-determination (Hart, 1996).

The Physical Space of the Classroom. Any adult learning environment needs to be aesthetically and culturally welcoming. The furniture and artwork need to be inviting and comfortable, and elders can be asked to assist in the design of this environment. I was reminded recently of the importance of environment when a Native teacher in a new high school in a Native community expressed dismay about the failure of her community to make the physical environment of her school welcoming. When elders came to her school to speak, they found the physical environment cold and uninviting; they felt uncomfortable. Involving elders in the planning of adult education spaces and inviting them to find a place there regularly contributes positively to the spiritual environment.

Ecological Worldview. Strategies that draw on stories of the elders such as *Keepers of the Earth* (Caduto and Bruchac, 1989), *Stories from the Six Worlds* (Whitehead, 1988), and *Voices of the First Nations* (Ahenakew, Gardipy, and Lafond, 1995) provide a way to keep social, scientific, and communication studies centered on an ecological worldview. The strategy of contrapuntal reading that was developed by postcolonial educators (Greenlaw, 1995) works well in helping adult learners compare Native perspectives with the perspectives of writers from the dominant society. This process requires adult learners to read texts that present voices from differing perspectives and to contrast the worldviews of the Native and dominant societies. This strategy provides Native adult learners with the opportunity to examine the limitations of a purely western worldview, and to gain insight about their own culture.

Story Circles. A way to facilitate story circles is to invite learners to write paragraphs and pass them around the circle for others to read and expand on. While this process encourages learners to build stories cooperatively, it also supports a relational form of learning that respects the importance of what all participants have to say; it also encourages collective ownership of circle stories.

Including the Elders. The wisdom of elders can be used to teach spirituality. Where possible, adult learners need to be engaged in activities that encourage them to interact with elders and hear their stories. Interviewing elders is a particularly useful process for developing a space for honoring their wisdom. Interviewing also develops the oral and literacy skills of adult learners. Rather than using traditional mainstream texts to reinforce literacy, adult learners can learn Native wisdom and values through Native texts as they develop communication skills. This activity can be engaged in by learners at all levels.

Where possible, adult learners should be encouraged to speak with elders about or in aboriginal languages, and to learn from their elders about the spiritual dimensions of their languages. A return to the languages of their ancestors is for many Natives a healing tool and a way to cultivate a spiritual identity (Battiste, 1998).

The Talking Circle. Using the talking circle is also a way to include the voices of participants in the learning process and to cultivate interpersonal knowing. Perhaps the most important dimension of talking circles is the space they create for all participants to listen unconditionally. Adult educators can facilitate the talking circle by asking participants to pass around a sacred object such as an eagle feather or a rock. All participants are invited to speak when they hold the sacred object, although speaking is an option, not a requirement, and to listen respectfully when others are speaking. I have found the talking circle to be particularly useful when introducing or developing highly sensitive topics, and for debriefing teaching processes and concepts. It is important to make sure that trust is carefully and thoroughly developed before this process is used so as not to trivialize this sacred teaching tool.

In my own practice as an adult educator, I have found that close attention to Native ways of knowing has made my teaching more spiritually rooted. By attending to the physical classroom environment, I respond better to the needs of my students and feel closer to them. By paying attention to the wisdom of elders and honoring both ecological dimensions and Native values, I am better able to address the complexity of the world in which my Native students live. By focusing my andragogical practice on relational ways of knowing, I have come to recognize a spiritual purpose for being, and my students—both Native and non-Native—have learned ways of being that honor and respect one another and all living things.

References

Ahenakew, F., Gardipy, B., and Lafond, B. *Voices of the First Nations.* Toronto; McGraw-Hill Ryerson, 1995.

Battiste, M. "Introduction." In M. Battiste and J. Barman (eds.), *First Nations Education in Canada: The Circle Unfolds.* Vancouver: University of British Columbia Press, 1995.

Battiste, M. "Enabling the Autumn Seed: Toward a Decolonized Approach to Aboriginal Knowledge, Language, and Education." *Canadian Journal of Native Education,* 1998, 22 (1), 16–27.

Caduto, M. J., and Bruchac, J. *Keepers of the Earth: Native Stories and Environmental Activities.* Saskatoon, Saskatchewan: Fifth House, 1989.

Calliou, S. "Peacekeeping Actions at Home: A Medicine Wheel for a Peacekeeping Pedagogy." In M. Battiste and J. Barman (eds.), *First Nations Education in Canada: The Circle Unfolds.* Vancouver: University of British Columbia Press, 1995.

Ermine, W. "Aboriginal Epistemology." In M. Battiste and J. Barman (eds.), *First Nations Education in Canada: The Circle Unfolds.* Vancouver: University of British Columbia Press, 1995.

Francis, B. *Voices from the Four Directions.* Closing remarks at the Second Annual L'nui'-sultnej: Let Us Speak Mi'Kmaq Language Conference, St. Francis Xavier University, Antigonish, Nova Scotia, June 5, 1999.

Friesen, D., and Orr, J. A. *Northern Aboriginal Teachers' Voices.* Saskatoon: Saskatchewan Teachers Federation, 1995.

Graveline, F. J. *Circle Works: Transforming Eurocentric Consciousness.* Halifax, Nova Scotia: Fernwood, 1998.

Greenlaw, J. C. "A Postcolonial Conception of the High School Multicultural Literature Curriculum." Research Report no. 95–05. Saskatoon, Saskatchewan: School Trustees Association, 1995.

Haig-Brown, C. "Taking Control: Contradiction and First Nations Adult Education." In M. Battiste and J. Barman (eds.), *First Nations Education in Canada: The Circle Unfolds.* Vancouver: University of British Columbia Press, 1995.

Hampton, E. "Towards a Redefinition of Indian Education." In M. Battiste and J. Barman (eds.), *First Nations Education in Canada: The Circle Unfolds.* Vancouver: University of British Columbia Press, 1995.

Hart, M. "Sharing Circles: Using Traditional Practise Methods for Teaching, Helping, and Supporting." In S. O'Meara and D. A. West (eds.), *From Our Eyes: Learning from Indigenous Peoples.* Toronto: Garamond Press, 1996.

Hart, M., and Holton, D. W. "Beyond God the Father and the Mother: Adult Education and Spirituality." In P. Jarvis and N. Walters (eds.), *Adult Education and Theological Interpretations.* Malabar, Fla.: Krieger, 1993.

Hill, D. *Aboriginal Access to Post-Secondary Education: Prior Learning Assessment and Its Use with Aboriginal Programs of Learning.* Desoronto, OH: First Nations Technical Institute, 1995.

Mander, J. *In the Absence of the Sacred: The Failure of Technology and the Survival of the Indian Nations.* San Francisco: Sierra Club Books, 1991.

Miller, J. R. *Skyscrapers Hide the Heavens.* Toronto: University of Toronto Press, 1991.

National Indian Brotherhood. *Indian Control of Indian Education.* Ottawa, Ontario: National Indian Brotherhood, 1972.

O'Meara, S., and West, D. A. (eds.). *From Our Eyes: Learning from Indigenous Peoples.* Toronto: Garamond Press, 1996.

Orr, D. W. *Ecological Literacy: Education and the Transition to a Postmodern World.* Albany, N.Y.: State University of New York Press, 1992.

Orr, J. A. "Mi'kmaq Women Educators' Life Histories: Implications for First Nations Education." Paper presented at the Canadian Society for the Study of Education, Ottawa, May 29, 1998.

Orr, J. A., and Friesen, D. "'I Think What Is Happening Is That We Are Taking Control': Aboriginal Teachers' Stories of Self-Determination." *Teachers and Teaching,* 1999, 5 (2), 219–241.

Powers, W. *Sacred Language: The Nature of Supernatural Discourse in Lakota.* Norman: University of Oklahoma Press, 1986.

Regnier, R. "The Sacred Circle: An Aboriginal Approach to Healing at an Urban High School." In M. Battiste and J. Barman (eds.), *First Nations Education in Canada: The Circle Unfolds.* Vancouver: University of British Columbia Press, 1995.

Ross, R. *Returning to the Teachings: Exploring Aboriginal Justice.* Toronto: Penguin, 1996.

Saskatchewan Department of Education. "Minister's Task Force Report on Northern Education." Regina, Saskatchewan: Saskatchewan Department of Education, 1989.

Sioui, G. "The Discovery of Americity." In G. McMaster and L. A. Martin (eds.), *Indigena: Contemporary Native Perspectives.* Vancouver, British Columbia: Douglas and McIntyre, 1992.

Slattery, P. *Curriculum Development in the Postmodern Era.* New York: Garland, 1995.

Snow, Chief John. *These Mountains Are Our Sacred Places.* Toronto: Samuel Stevens, 1977.

Whitehead, R. H. *Stories from the Six Worlds: Micmac Legends.* Halifax, Nova Scotia: Nimbus, 1988.

Jeffrey A. Orr is associate professor and chair of the Department of Education, St. Francis Xavier University, Antigonish, Nova Scotia, Canada.

7

This chapter describes two cases in which community development, adult education, and spirituality have been interwoven. The author uses these cases to make suggestions for adult education practice.

Community Development and Adult Education: Locating Practice in Its Roots

Wilf E. Bean

In the 1920s, Lindeman ([1926] 1961) wrote that the aim of adult education was the creation of meaning out of life experience. This purpose, in secular terms, was often defined as spiritual. In Lindeman's view, the meaning gained through adult education was not complete until it was expressed in social action.

For thousands of years, social activists, educators, and religious leaders had shared the assumption that all citizens of the world should have the opportunity to develop socially, morally, and politically, and to benefit economically from the earth's bounty. All people's lives should have meaning. The ideals of justice, service, caring, cooperation, and the dignity of the person were fundamental to the work of many adult educators and community workers. These transcendent ideals gave such workers both inner, spiritual understanding and a social purpose. Their motivations went beyond money and individual status. They viewed themselves as contributing to a greater, social cause.

However, with the post–Second World War rise in the development of industry and with the professionalization of both adult education and development, it has become less fashionable to speak of spiritual ideals, or even to ask how one's work contributes to the greater well-being of humanity. Although many adult educators and development workers genuinely try to contribute to a lasting, greater good, it is clear that much activity in the name of development does not seriously concern itself with such questions. Projects are often judged only in terms of efficiency, economic impact, and more recently, the level of gender participation. Long-term impact, when considered, seldom involves more than five years.

Fortunately, throughout the world there are examples where a significantly different approach is courageously undertaken. One good example is that of the women and men in the Chipko Movement in northern India who literally hugged the trees when they became aware of the fact that deforestation was destabilizing the hillsides and destroying the forests they considered sacred. Another example is base Christian communities in Latin America, where thousands of marginalized and middle-class women and men gather in small groups to reflect and act on their community concerns in the light of biblical texts. Still another example is the revitalization of many North American First Nations peoples through the reconstruction and evolution of traditional practices of spirituality and organization. In the previous chapter, Orr tells us that the act of communion with the earth, which is so basic to Native ways of knowing, is also basic to all spiritual development.

In each of these cases, there is congruence between inner, spiritual understandings and collective action. A vision of justice and "right relations" motivates people to come together so that both individually and collectively they may contribute to making this vision a reality.

The two examples I consider in this chapter come from different times and contexts, but they have many similarities. After describing these examples, I conclude with some thoughts on a contemporary adult education practice of spirituality and development for North Americans based on a set of principles.

The Antigonish Movement, Canada

When Moses Coady and Jimmy Tompkins began their community development–adult education approach to community awareness and the formation of cooperatives in eastern Nova Scotia, Canada, the underlying concern was not simply the creation of study clubs, cooperatives, or even economic development. The motivating vision was more spiritual: to bring life to all the people (Laidlaw, 1971). In his speeches, Coady set forth a vision in which each man and woman would participate fully in bringing about this new life. He spoke of a world crying for genuine democracy for all people, but insisted this would not happen with guns, armies, or bombs. Rather, his vision was about people and their participation, not only politically, but also in the economic, social, and educational forces that shaped them. Through a process of adult education and group action, he envisioned people gaining power over their own affairs (MacLellan, 1985).

Although this vision, which later became known as the Antigonish Movement, challenged men and women throughout the region to become involved in rebuilding their society, Coady knew there were strong forces opposing truly democratic institutions. He did not hesitate to name big business, banks, and finance as the real problems, and he saw their ruthless activities as similar to those that Christ had denounced as life destroying. Coady summoned the people of Nova Scotia to follow Christ's example of challenging injustice and urged them to be prepared to defy unjust relations locally (Laidlaw, 1971).

The underlying principle of social justice permeated Coady's and Tompkins's understanding of community development and adult education, and justified their actions as they encouraged the disadvantaged to organize into cooperatives and credit unions, both locally and regionally. They both acknowledged community groups as absolutely essential, but they knew that lasting social change would require more than study clubs and savings groups to bring about lasting social change. This shift in power would require the people to control their own social and economic institutions. The program of adult education and economic cooperation they developed was the means for this deeper principle to be manifested, a principle that informed both inner and outer life (Alexander, 1997; Lotz and Welton, 1987, 1997). Chapter Three in this volume, by Leona English, refers to this type of program as *informal learning,* and highlights the mentoring strategy that Coady and Tompkins used so successfully.

Spirituality, for Coady, was inseparable from life in the material world (Gillen, 1998). It was not just an individual, interior phenomenon of feeling good, but it required expression through action in the world. Just as materialism erred in failing to recognize a reality beyond the material world, so too there was error in failing to recognize that spirituality must be made manifest in action. In recalling the biblical parable of the Good Samaritan, Coady noted that Jesus explained the meaning of true spirituality through the material actions of stopping for the wounded traveler, binding his wounds, and giving cash to the innkeeper for his care. In other words, it was only through the visible that the invisible could be seen.

As a Roman Catholic priest, Coady's insistence on the consistency between principles and practice led him to challenge the lifestyle of his fellow priests. When they lobbied the bishop for good homes with bathrooms, Coady did not hesitate to point out that if such amenities were not available to people in the communities, they should not be available to the priests (Laidlaw, 1971).

Coady's vision of social justice led him to question position, privilege, and the responsibility of leadership, both locally and globally. In his view, a leader must be with, not above, the people. The people themselves, not the leaders, through programs of adult education and group action, would be the ones who would build the new society.

Coady emphasized the common right of all people to the resources of the earth. But consistently his vision was both material and spiritual. For him, the fulfillment of people's cultural and spiritual lives was inseparable from the right use and distribution of the world's resources.

Sarvodaya Shramadana, Sri Lanka

Movements of spirituality, adult education, and community development have emerged in various parts of the world. Just as the Antigonish Movement developed within the region's Christian framework, in Sri Lanka a community-based adult education movement emerged within Buddhism and brought about an awakening of the people there.

In 1959, the year Moses Coady died, a small group of Sri Lankan high school teachers and students concerned about the country's rural poor organized a volunteer rural work camp. This experience inspired them to take action. Under the leadership of A. T. Ariyaratne they proceeded to foster a community development–adult education movement of enlightenment and action based on the Buddhist principles of loving-kindness, equanimity, compassion, and equality. Today, although it faces the challenge of organizational development to cope with growth (Lean, 1995), the movement reaches more than eight thousand villages, about a third of the villages in the nation.

Just as the Antigonish Movement emphasized that meaningful development must combine spirituality, adult education, and social change, so does the Sarvodaya Shramadana Movement. The name itself combines both spiritual and social change elements, joining familiar, traditional phrases in a new way. Mahatama Gandhi coined the word *sarvodaya;* it means "the awakening of us all." *Shramadana* is the practice of voluntary sharing of time, resources, ideas, energy, and labor. Taken together, the movement's name emphasizes enlightenment through service and sharing (Ariyaratne, n.d.).

Following Buddhist understandings, Sarvodaya Shramadana emphasizes the interconnectedness of reality. It calls for awakening at four levels: the personal, the village, the nation, and the world, beginning with the poorest villagers. Achievements are measured not just in changes in social systems or economic production, but also in human transformation. An underlying assumption of the movement is that development must be meaningful in terms of human fulfillment. Although the systems of production and consumption of goods must be changed, the movement entails much more, including the unfolding of the villagers' potential for wisdom and compassion (Macy, 1988).

The movement is organized around a systematic five-stage approach of community education. The principles of service and self-reliance are fundamental. In the first stage, a village requests a Sarvodaya worker, perhaps along with a volunteer from another village that has undergone an awakening process. After some discussion, the villagers are challenged to take responsibility for identifying and organizing a shramadana, or shared labor project, to meet a village need that has been agreed upon. Such projects might, for example, involve road improvement, cleaning wells, or latrine construction. Over a period of a month or two, the work camp is organized, with the involvement of many villagers through various local task forces (Macy, 1988).

In stage two, some of these task forces evolve into functional groups, according to the needs of individuals and the community—for example, mothers, youth, elders, children, or farmers. Training is planned to meet the group's needs, such as organizing mothers for a particular task or perhaps providing farmers with specific technical skills relating to agriculture or bookkeeping.

In stage three, a village Sarvodaya Society is legally incorporated, thus formalizing the planning and coordination process within the community. The groups continue to define their needs and organize and undertake projects, but increasingly they consider the common well-being of all. Economic and employment projects increase.

The fourth stage emphasizes the sustainability of the village through the strengthening of income-generating activities along with continuing social development. By the fifth stage, the community has matured to where it can offer services or economic surplus to other, less-developed villages. At this point, the village is encouraged to consider its regional, national, and international interdependence and to contribute, within its ability to do so, to the greater awakening at these levels.

Throughout this five-stage process, villagers are challenged to reflect on both the reality of the village and on their own individual lives. Real social change requires personal change, and villagers are encouraged to consider changes in their own lives as part of the changing web of village relationships. Only in this way can there be fundamental, lasting changes at both levels.

However, just as Moses Coady recognized strong forces of opposition to people gaining greater control over their own institutions, so does Sarvodaya Shramadana. Opposing internal and external forces are identified at each level—the individual, the village, and the nation. At the village level, internal forces may include conflict, exploitation, and distrust among villagers themselves. External forces may be absentee landowners, moneylenders, middlemen, and traders. Both inner and outer constraints must be removed in order for awakening to take place (Ariyaratne, n.d.).

Ariyaratne insisted that it is only the people themselves who can overcome these forces. In this way, he echoed the challenge that Moses Coady put to the people of eastern Nova Scotia. Although the expressions differ because of different cultural, religious, and geographical contexts, both movements are based on a fundamental, even radical respect for the dignity and capacity of all persons to make changes in their lives, beginning with those who are most disadvantaged. In both movements, the philosophy and practice do not encourage a rugged individualism that separates and alienates, but rather a greater capacity for group action for the common good.

A Spirituality in Development for Our Times

If North Americans are to develop a contemporary practice of adult education and community development that brings life to the people, then it must come from an understanding and practice grounded in reality. The task is not easy, in part because the essential words themselves carry immense baggage. At best, *spirituality* is a vague term encompassing a vast landscape of meaning. For some, it connotes only passivity, inner life, or otherworldly matters. For others, it carries the weight of unredeemable, patriarchal religions. For some, the term connotes a disconnected individualism, that unique part of oneself that is most private, most distant from others, having little to do with collective action; others see it as having an outward thrust. It may scare away as many people as it attracts. Similarly, there is no clear consensus about the meaning of the term *development* (Chambers, 1997; Sachs, 1992).

Present labels for spirituality may be inadequate, but there remains within us a need for meaning, for understanding how our lives fit into the larger world. Although this need is certainly not the only one we experience, it gives rise to a number of concerns, such as the suffering of others and a desire to alleviate that suffering when possible. Then there is the matter of building a world that provides for the greater fulfillment of all people. Regardless of the words used, these needs, concerns, and matters can be the basis for the construction of a contemporary spirituality and community development practice.

There are also contributing social forces at play in today's world. The global ecological crisis challenges us to rethink our relationship with the natural world. New information technologies connect us globally, both helping us to recognize our common humanity and, arguably, creating greater awareness of the vast and growing global inequalities. Within our rapidly changing, fragmented societies there is a growing search for deeper truths and wholeness through a renewed interest in spirituality.

In this time of transformation, how can adult educators and community development workers respond? Let me suggest some principles that will help to foster a contemporary spirituality and make it relevant. For each principle, I provide examples drawn from associated adult education and community development practices.

Spiritual Principle 1: Ecological Base. Humans are not the apex of creation but one species within a complex, interdependent web of life. All creation is sacred. Humans must learn to live responsibly and interdependently within the limits of a sustainable, natural environment or, as a species, humanity will not survive. Many researchers and theologians are exploring this dimension of a new spirituality (Berry, 1992; Hallman, 1994; McFague, 1997; Ó Murchú, 1998; Ruether, 1992).

Application: Clover and Follen (1998) are developing an adult education approach that combines popular education with environmental principles.

The workshops she conducts in natural settings encourage greater awareness, appreciation, and analysis of the environment and of the threats posed to it. Participants may, for example, collect local soil samples or other natural objects that symbolize their connectedness to nature. They then create plays, songs, poems, and stories as ways of sharing with others the issues facing the environment. Through reflection and analysis, these issues are analyzed within a larger, gender-sensitive, political, economic framework. With this new understanding, participants then make plans for appropriate actions.

Spiritual Principle 2: Social Justice. The increasing global exploitation of both humans and nature is unjust. German theologian Ulrich Duchrow (1987) calls the present global economy our greatest theological issue. Although Western society may see itself as secular, John McMurtry (1998) says that in fact free-market capitalism has become its religion. The global market is like a god, the unknowable, unseen force shaping reality. Citizens are asked to accept on faith the fact that reward and punishment, the means of life and death, will be justly dispensed at some future time according to their willingness to sacrifice today.

Application: In our educational programs for adults at the Coady International Institute, an outgrowth of the Antigonish Movement, we begin a global analysis by having participants inspect the labels on their clothes. Where did the material come from? Where was it sewn? By whom? Under what conditions? At what hourly rate? Where was it sold? At what cost? How many people have been involved in producing the article? Who benefited most overall? A similar exercise can be conducted with food. Deborah Barndt (1996) has developed an analysis of global food production based on an examination of Tomasita Tomato, a fictional character who originates in Mexico and ends up in a Canadian kitchen. From such examples, an awareness of both the structural or more permanent and conjunctural or short-term economic, political, and social forces can be developed (Barndt, 1989). Within the practice of community economic development, educators have developed other exercises, such as *Ah-Hah* (Gatt-Fly, 1983) and the *Leaky Bucket* (Fairbairn and others, 1991) as a way to analyze the flow of wealth, power, goods, and services into and out of communities. On the basis of these analyses, participants reflect on the underlying values on which these systems are based.

Spiritual Principle 3: The Dignity of the Human Person. Each person is a unique "Subject," a creator and an end in himself or herself, not an object to be used for the benefit of others. This understanding can be extended to the natural world by recognizing the inherent rights of all life forms, human and nonhuman (McFague, 1997). In general, this principle requires the transformation of relations of domination and oppression, both globally and locally. It challenges hierarchies and bureaucracies that fail to recognize the full humanity of all.

Application: In the first chapter of this volume, Vella describes an approach to adult education based on a "spirited epistemology" that respects the learner as Subject. In our work at the Coady International Institute, this principle underlies the reason we encourage people's organizations—that is, member-owned institutions such as cooperatives, women's organizations, and worker's unions that are controlled by members for their own benefit. In our educational practice, we recognize the dignity of each person in various ways, such as through the use of "rounds," which give each participant a voice during a process of reflection or evaluation, and also through exercises such as drawing and sharing "life-lines" or "rivers of life" (Hope and Timmel, 1992, p. 35). To respect the dignity of the person, we encourage participants to set their own limits during such personal exercises, and to pass during rounds if such a decision makes them feel more comfortable.

Spiritual Principle 4: Community Based. "I am because we are," says the African Xhosa proverb. An individual's life both is shaped by and in turn shapes the web of relationships of which it is a part. Although each life is part of a larger whole, a Western hyperindividualist culture often makes it difficult to work cooperatively and with care and respect. Without this capacity, it is difficult to transform either the larger society or the individual person.

Application: At the Coady International Institute, we consider small groups to be essential building blocks for any grassroots social-change movement. Much of our education is within small groups. Through training workshops, we encourage the development of various human-relations skills, including group facilitation, decision making, reflection, and conflict resolution. In this way, participants increase their capacity to be effective members and mobilizers of small groups.

Spiritual Principle 5: Action for Liberation. A spirituality for development is not simply an understanding or a pleasant emotional state. It is the practice of justice, of choosing life over death, of "setting the captive free." It is the practice of working for the transformation of conditions of exploitation, oppression, and limitation of the fullness of life wherever we find such barriers (Gutierrez, 1973; Harris, 1996; Rumscheidt, 1998).

Application: Questions such as "How can you apply this principle to your work?" or "What actions can you take as a result of your new understanding?" can lead to implementation and action. Our adult education workshops normally conclude with action-planning sessions in which participants decide how to implement their learning.

Spiritual Principle 6: Combined Action and Reflection. This profound adult education principle is relevant both for the groups with whom adult educators work and for adult educators and development workers themselves. Palmer (1990) suggests that it is by embracing both the active and contemplative sides of our nature that we develop the capacity to express our deepest inner convictions and truths through our actions. Whatever the results, our actions nevertheless are consistent with our deeper sustaining truth.

Application: Meetings and educational events can include time for silence and thoughtful reflection. Workshops and retreats specifically for social change workers are helpful in preventing and overcoming the burnout, polarization, and wounds often associated with this work. Such events encourage personal reflection and spiritual growth without denying the importance of social engagement.

These spiritual principles do not stand separately. Each is a strand in a larger, interconnected vision of a more sustainable, equitable world in which both people and resources are honored as sacred and where everyone is more fulfilled through an increased awareness of their connection and contribution to the greater good of the entire Earth community. This is a vision in which spirituality, adult education, and development are inseparable, and one that challenges adult educators and development workers to understand their work as central to the project of human betterment.

References

Alexander, A. *The Antigonish Movement: Moses Coady and Adult Education Today.* Toronto: Thompson Educational Publishing, 1997.

Ariyaratne, A. T. *Collected Works.* Vol. 1. (N. Ratnapala, ed.). Dehiwala, Sri Lanka: Sarvodaya Research Institute, n.d.

Barndt, D. *Naming the Moment: Political Analysis for Education: A Manual for Community Groups.* Toronto: Jesuit Centre for Social Faith and Justice, 1989.

Barndt, D. "Tracing the Trail of Tomasita Tomato: Popular Education Around Globalization." *Alternatives Journal,* 1996, 22 (1), 24–29.

Berry, T. *Befriending the Earth: A Theology of Reconciliation Between Humans and the Earth.* Mystic, Conn.: Twenty-Third Publications, 1992.

Chambers, R. *Whose Reality Counts? Putting the First Last.* London: Intermediate Technology, 1997.

Clover, D., and Follen, S. *Case Studies in Environmental Adult and Popular Education.* Toronto: LEAP/International Council for Adult Education, 1998.

Duchrow, U. *Global Economy: A Confessional Issue for the Churches.* Geneva: World Council of Churches Publications, 1987.

Fairbairn, B., and others. *Co-operatives and Community Development: Economics in Social Perspective.* Saskatoon: Centre for the Study of Co-operatives, University of Saskatchewan, 1991.

Gatt-Fly. *Ah-Hah! A New Approach to Popular Education.* Toronto: Between the Lines, 1983.

Gillen, M. A. "Spiritual Lessons from the Antigonish Movement." In S. Scott, B. Spencer, and A. Thomas (eds.), *Learning for Life: Canadian Readings in Adult Education.* Toronto: Thompson Educational Publishing, 1998.

Gutierrez, G. *A Theology of Liberation: History, Politics and Salvation.* Maryknoll, N.Y.: Orbis Books, 1973.

Hallman, D. (ed.). *Ecotheology: Voices from South and North.* Geneva, Switzerland: World Council of Churches Publications, 1994.

Harris, M. *Proclaim Jubilee: A Spirituality for the Twenty-First Century.* Louisville, Ky.: Westminster/John Knox Press, 1996.

Hope, A., and Timmel, S. *Training for Transformation: A Handbook for Community Workers.* Book 2. Gweru, Zimbabwe: Mambo Press, 1992.

Laidlaw, A. (ed.). *The Man from Margaree: Writing and Speeches of M. M. Coady.* Toronto: McClelland and Stewart, 1971.

Lean, M. *Bread, Bricks, and Belief: Communities in Charge of Their Future.* West Hartford, Conn.: Kumarian Press, 1995.

Lindeman, E. C. *The Meaning of Adult Education.* Montreal: Harvest House, 1961. (Originally published 1926.)

Lotz, J., and Welton, M. "Knowledge for the People: The Life and Times of the Antigonish Movement." In M. Welton (ed.), *Knowledge for the People: The Struggle for Adult Learning in English-Speaking Canada, 1823–1973.* Toronto: OISE Press, 1987.

Lotz, J., and Welton, M. *Father Jimmy: The Life and Times of Father Jimmy Tompkins.* Wreck Cove, Nova Scotia: Breton Books, 1997.

MacLellan, M. *Coady Remembered.* Antigonish, Nova Scotia: St. Francis Xavier University Press, 1985.

Macy, J. *Dharma and Development: Religion as Resource in the Sarvodaya Self-Help Movement.* West Hartford, Conn.: Kumarian Press, 1988.

McFague, S. *Super, Natural Christians: How We Should Love Nature.* Minneapolis: Augsburg Fortress, 1997.

McMurtry, J. *Unequal Freedoms: The Global Market as an Ethical System.* Toronto: Garamond Press, 1998.

Ó Murchú, D. *Reclaiming Spirituality.* New York: Crossroad, 1998.

Palmer, P. J. *The Active Life: Wisdom for Work, Creativity and Caring.* San Francisco: Harper San Francisco, 1990.

Ruether, R. R. *Gaia and God: An Ecofeminist Theology of Earth Healing.* San Francisco: Harper San Francisco, 1992.

Rumscheidt, B. *No Room for Grace: Pastoral Theology and Dehumanization in the Global Economy.* Grand Rapids, Mich.: Eerdmans, 1998.

Sachs, W. *The Development Dictionary: A Guide to Knowledge as Power.* London: Zed Books, 1992.

WILF E. BEAN is a staff member of the Coady International Institute, St. Francis Xavier University, Antigonish, Nova Scotia, Canada.

8

Lay ministry education programs attend to the spiritual dimension of their participants' growth whenever principles of adult education are applied. This chapter describes one such program and how its components nourish the spiritual development of its participants.

The Spiritual Dimensions of Lay Ministry Programs

Catherine P. Zeph

There is an increasing awareness of spirituality in North America today that is finding expression both outside of and within traditional religious institutions. For centuries, formal religions have provided rituals, traditions, and institutional beliefs for individuals and communities who seek a spiritual understanding of life's questions. However, the changing societal and global transformations of recent years have led growing numbers of adults to seek spiritual answers to their questions outside of formal religious institutions (Ó Murchú, 1998).

This search is evident in countless and creative ways outside of traditional religious institutions. Ancient traditional forms of spiritual meditations such as the labyrinth walk or centering prayer are being reclaimed; spiritual practices from various traditions are being explored and integrated, intentional communities are being organized, twelve-step support groups have formed for all kinds of needs, retreat centers are booming, philosophy and theology groups are using study circles to learn about the wisdom of the ages, and people are becoming aware of the spiritual benefits of connecting with the natural world through outdoor activity and meditation (Van Ness, 1996). The encounter with the creative mystery of the divine is also being expressed more explicitly in such ways as journaling, painting, pottery, playing or listening to music, dreamwork, counseling, and bodywork. These many informal and voluntary expressions of the spiritual search are solid, accepted, and renewed forms of the classic spiritual search (Brussat and Brussat, 1998).

At the same time, there is also a growing interest in spirituality within traditional religious settings. Programs for religious and lay ministry education are being offered within local churches and universities, at retreat centers and distance education sites, through the Internet, and in the home. Whether they be informal adult education meetings focused on prayer, structured denominational inquiry classes, retreats or lectures, or the rigors of a graduate degree program, these programs might be regarded as another response to the hunger for spirituality that is prevalent in our culture today. This chapter provides an overview on these programs, presents one case study of a graduate degree program developed for lay ministry education, and reflects on how, through the use of good adult education principles, these programs can nourish spiritual growth in their participants.

Lay Ministry

For centuries, institutional churches have provided education for their ordained and religious members, first through monasteries and convents, and later through seminaries and universities. Worshiping communities of all denominations and faiths recognize the value of developing their members' spirituality. For example, the Jewish adult education literature (Rohfeld and Zachary, 1995; Zachary, 1992) reports a growth in programs related to Jewish spirituality and traditions, similar to those developed in Christian circles. Today, Jews have an increased interest in learning about their faith and historical culture, whether individually, at the local synagogue, or in formal programs of continuing and higher education. And as with many adult education programs today, there is an interest in more process-oriented or learner-centered learning. According to Zachary and Burstyn (1993), "Today the Rabbi is seen as a teacher, not *the* teacher, of adults" (p. 13). Katz (1998) provides a contemporary overview of adult Jewish education programming that is delivered in community settings, and provides ideas for revitalizing and strengthening this kind of education. The aims of Jewish adult education are nurturing faith, providing information, and preserving history. Christian adult education has similar aims, along with the additional focus of fostering the baptismal call to ministry.

In this chapter, I take a slightly different direction, focusing on Christian lay ministry education programs in North America because I am familiar with such programs. This decision also limits the scope of this discussion. Although the idea of lay ministry may be generalized to all faiths, its specific roots as a known practice are embedded and intrinsic to the Christian Church. As a term, *lay ministry* is not part of the Jewish tradition nor of other religious traditions. Within the Christian Church, ministry is not simply a privilege of the ordained but rather a responsibility of all who are baptized, and it "is always ordered toward the service of others" (Bernier, 1992, p. 284). Toward this end, churches locally and nationally offer programs in lay ministry education as a way to educate and spiritually nourish the life of their members.

The Profession of Ministry

Professional groups generally have a common understanding of a certain body of knowledge relating to practice and they assert some measure of privilege and power (Houle, 1980). Ministers, doctors, lawyers, and farmers learn not only the academics of their profession but also the skills needed to practice and perform their work (Coll, 1992). As in other professions, the term *lay* within the ministry profession refers to those who are not part of the ordained profession, to those who are not credentialed or skilled and who are thought of as commonfolk. Yet in the case of ministry, the term has its roots in this very profession. The word *lay* comes from the Greek word *laikos*, or "people," and in general it is used to describe those who are not ordained ministers. For many centuries, ordained ministers were the ones who received an education and therefore were considered to be the elite; they were vested with power within the Church. Kenan Osborne (1993) provides a rich historical overview of the profession of ministry and explains that in the early middle ages, the lack of educated lay Christians was the main reason they were depositioned within the church. This educational and therefore professional division within the ministry has remained somewhat throughout the centuries. Ordained ministers have usually been considered to be *the* church professionals. Today, lay ministers are being educated and acknowledged as professionals, although some tensions and differences related to different professionalization experiences still remain (Fox, 1997).

Lay ministry as a career is attracting those who, by virtue of gender or marriage, cannot be ordained, or those who do not desire ordination or preaching roles but wish to work within the ministry profession (for instance, as religious educators, liturgists, musicians, pastoral administrators, spiritual directors, grief counselors, social justice workers, and other such roles that do not necessarily need the prescribed training of those seeking to preach or perform sacramental rites). For many, the work of ministry is a way of seeking and sharing their faith with others (Fox, 1997). It is a way of committing to the common good that Linda Vogel speaks about in Chapter Two.

For all of these reasons, enrollment in lay ministry programs has been increasing. These programs welcome not only students who seek professional ministerial roles but also those who wish to further their spiritual growth consciously through the academic study of theology and ministry. It is on these types of professional lay ministry programs that I focus in the rest of this chapter.

Lay Ministry Programs

Like many other professional programs, lay ministry programs often focus on the acquisition of content subject matter and the practice of some skill development, so they may not require (though they may strongly encourage) their students to engage in spiritual development as part of their academic preparation.

Participants. Unlike many traditional professional programs that attract young adults right out of college, lay ministry education programs tend to attract middle-aged adults, typically between the ages of thirty-five and fifty (Fleischer, 1997). Most students seek to become better prepared or credentialed as ministers, while others enroll as a means toward spiritual enrichment. Recent surveys show that the average participants in these programs are "white women in their early middle age, married and becoming educated in theology" (Horan, 1998, p. 263). Although these professional programs are academic and their explicit purpose is to prepare students for ministry, a profession that springs from and is responsive to the needs of the church, they frequently do not attend to the spiritual needs of their students (Fox, 1997).

Spirituality. Spirituality, as it has been described in the Editors' Notes of this volume, refers to an awareness of something greater than ourselves, a sense that we are connected to and in relationship with all human beings in community and with all of creation. In the profession of ministry, ministers assist others through service and leadership. Their aim is to nurture these relationships via an expressed relationship with the divine. In Christian terms, this relationship is expressed through the personage and divinity of Jesus Christ, who called people to live in relationship through community. Parker J. Palmer (1983) notes that historically the three disciplines within the monastic communal life were the study of scripture, prayer, and the gathering of community. These three disciplines may be found, explicitly or implicitly, in many contemporary professional lay ministry programs.

Components of Programs. Lay education programs that encourage and nourish the spiritual development of their students are grounded in solid adult education principles that integrate three key components: critical reflection, the integration of one's own life and ministerial experience with academic study, and the explicit invitation to do this within a learning community. Within this learning community, students are provided the space in which to share with others and to begin integrating their critical reflections about themselves, their experiences, and their studies in a disciplined and loving environment. In many ways, this is what the students will be called to do as ministers. The learning community provides them with an opportunity to be initiated into the practice of their profession.

The kind of critical reflection that the community life of these programs requires emanates from two key adult education principles: the learner is central, and ministry always takes place within a context (as does any kind of professional practice). Ultimately, the success of these programs is rooted in a spirited epistemology, and in the fact that adults come to learning situations with prior life experiences, with differing responsibilities and roles (such as student, spouse, employee, parent, and citizen), and with a commitment to learn; and they are of a certain chronological age, gender, race, and religious belief. Within the adult learning context, their experience is highly valued and is integral to how they make meaning in their lives.

Example of a Lay Ministry Program

The Loyola Institute for Ministry Extension (LIMEX) program is one such program that asks students, within an academically rigorous program, to reflect critically on what they are studying by integrating their life and ministerial experiences into their studies, and to do so within an intentional learning community. Originating at the Loyola Institute for Ministry at Loyola University, New Orleans, LIMEX is a distance education program that currently operates in at least twenty-five states and five countries (the United States, Canada, Scotland, England, and Switzerland). It is the largest lay education program within the Roman Catholic tradition in North America and has its roots in its Episcopalian counterpart, Education for Ministry (EFM), which is based at The University of the South in Sewanee, Tennessee. EFM operates in most states in the United States, in Canada, and in a number of other countries. Both of these programs are structured similarly and much of what is true about LIMEX could be said about EFM (see Killen, 1983, and EFM's Web site [http://www.sewanee.edu/EFM/EFMhome.html]). In the following discussion, I focus on LIMEX.

Structure of the Program. Working in partnership with a local sponsoring diocese or other religious institution, LIMEX offers master's degrees and certificates in religious education and pastoral studies by extension. Unlike many distance education programs, which enroll individual students who study alone and correspond with individual faculty via Internet or e-mail, the students in LIMEX study together in intentional learning groups that are facilitated by individuals who have prior experience as facilitators and are trained in group dynamics. Each learning group proceeds through twelve courses: each course comprises ten three-hour sessions that are designed to promote intellectual knowledge and critical reflection. Throughout each course, students dialogue in small and large groups, read printed lectures and textbooks, view videotapes of scholars and practitioners, and are asked to record their reflections in personal journals on an ongoing basis. They provide one another with feedback on their group participation and write papers that draw on their life experiences. Course assignments require students to integrate their assigned readings with their own life and ministerial experiences and with what they have shared and experienced in their learning group. This critical reflection on, engagement with, and integration of their own lives and coursework is essential to their professional development as ministers.

Intentional Learning Group. At the initial orientation session that explains the adult learning model and group structure of LIMEX, students are asked to read, reflect on, discuss, and then individually sign a learning group agreement that is sent to Loyola. As Wickett describes in Chapter

Four of this volume, the learning agreement or covenant ensures that participants are aware of the importance of the learning community, both for their own intellectual growth and for the healthy life of the group. The group agreement contains statements that direct attention to responsibility, relationship, communication, preparation, and recognition of growing in faith. Through this intentional learning group, students in the LIMEX program are able not only to dialogue about ideas and challenge each other safely, but also to practice the skills they need to become effective ministers who can attend to the spiritual development of themselves and their group. Ministry is not only about listening and responding, hearing different experiences and not judging, but also about helping others to make meaning out of their life experiences and relationships. If in the life of a learning group the dynamics sour or become stuck, the group is asked to review their learning group agreement and try to work out difficulties in an honest and loving manner. If difficulties persist, they call on their local liaison or a Loyola faculty member for assistance.

Critical Reflection. A four-step reflection process is used in the LIMEX program, based on two books by Bernard Lonergan, a Canadian Jesuit: *Insight* (1957) and *Method in Theology* (1972). Students are asked to identify an experience, to name their initial understanding of the experience, to judge or test their interpretations of the experience, and finally to decide what their next steps will be, based on the new information gained through the reflective process. As they reflect, students are asked to examine their ministry using four explicit contexts in which they operate: their own Christian tradition, their sociocultural context, the institutional contexts in which they are working, and their own personal context (life experiences that identify who they are). Students write their papers and dialogue with one another using this reflection process. For many students, this process becomes a basic toolkit with which to approach various situations in their ministries, workplaces, and personal lives.

Connections to Adult Education and Spirituality

Much has already been written in this volume about the spiritual dimensions of adult education. What is of particular relevance to the educational model used in the LIMEX program is the critical thinking and reflection components, which can lead to what Jack Mezirow (1991) refers to as *perspective transformation*. Mezirow's perspective transformation process is similar to Lonergan's (1957, 1972) four-step reflection process: both describe the movement from identifying and understanding oneself and one's world to reflecting critically on these understandings and then to making new choices or actions based on these reflections. LIMEX, as an adult-centered educational program, also incorporates many other concepts of good adult learning. The components of self-directed learning, intentional learning, collaborative learning, problem-centered learning, and action-reflection are all embedded in the structure of LIMEX. By taking students out of the traditional teacher-student roles and forcing them to open up to resources within and around themselves in ways that the traditional classroom does not, LIMEX encourages students to experience deeply the power of discovering and integrating their own life and professional histories with their studies; it is a way for them to reckon with their spiritual lives.

Henri Nouwen (1975) wrote about tending to the spiritual needs of students, particularly within the formal educational setting: "It seems that the least-used source of formation and information is the experience of the students themselves" (p. 59). He wrote about the need to create space for listening in classrooms and the need for relationships through community: "It is in these situations that we reach out to each other . . . and discover each other as a part of a larger community with a common destination" (p. 71). The learning community model that LIMEX and other programs emulate appears to be an appropriate learning model in which to nourish the spiritual dimensions of students' lives.

If spirituality is about realizing the connections between others and creation, is there a better place to help students realize these connections than through the formation of a learning group rooted in community? Jarvis (1993) believes that "for most people, seeking to understand the meaning of their existence is an intermittent but lifelong quest" (p. 100). If spirituality is about this search for answers to life's questions by cultivating a relationship with the divine, then it makes sense that the LIMEX program and others like it can offer participants the opportunity to grow spiritually themselves. The need for answers to life's questions can also help us understand the increased popularity of such programs, and why people find themselves transformed as they work together in these learning communities.

I have heard from countless students how their lives have been transformed by their participation in the LIMEX program, which seemingly occurs within the supportive atmosphere of their learning community when they realize the connections between the required academics and their own experiences. In reference to LIMEX, Barbara Fleischer (1997) notes that "only when new content and viewpoints are put in dialogue with a person's experience will transformation take place as an educational outcome" (p. 14).

As an adult educator, I believe that critical reflection is essential to the cultivation of spiritual dimensions of adult development in lay ministry education programs. The LIMEX program and others like it apply good adult learning principles and nourish their students' spiritual development through a learning community. The use of a learning community can model for participants a relationship with others and with all of creation that can foster a relationship with the divine. Innovative programs, whether within or outside traditional church settings, that include some sense of a learning community, critical reflection, and the integration of both studies and life experiences can foster the spiritual development of the adult learner.

References

Bernier, P. *Ministry in the Church: A Historical and Pastoral Approach.* Mystic, Conn.: Twenty-Third Publications, 1992.

Brussat, F., and Brussat, M. A. *Spiritual Literacy: Reading the Sacred in Everyday Life.* New York: Touchstone, 1998.

Coll, R. *Supervision of Ministry Students.* Collegeville, Minn.: Liturgical Press, 1992.

Fleischer, B. (ed.). *Introduction to Practical Theology: Ministry in Contexts.* New Orleans: Loyola Institute for Ministry, Loyola University New Orleans, 1997.

Fox, Z. *New Ecclesial Ministry: Lay Professionals Serving the Church.* Kansas City, Mo.: Sheed and Ward, 1997.

Horan, M. P. "Lay Pastoral Theology: Fostering Spiritual Adulthood in a Priest-Short Church." *The Way,* 1998, *30* (3), 260–270.

Houle, C. O. *Continuing Learning in the Professions.* San Francisco: Jossey-Bass, 1980.

Jarvis, P. "Meaning, Being, and Learning." In P. Jarvis and N. Walters (eds.), *Adult Education and Theological Interpretations.* Malabar, Fla.: Krieger, 1993.

Katz, B. D. "Community Based Adult Learning: The More Torah, the More Life. Pirke Avot 2:7." In Tornberg, R. E. (ed.), *The Jewish Educational Leader's Handbook.* Denver, Colo.: Alternatives in Religious Education, 1998.

Killen, D. P. "Theological Reflection: A Necessary Skill in Lay Ministry." In F. R. Kinsler (ed.), *Ministry by the People: Theological Education by Extension.* Geneva, Switzerland: World Council of Churches; and Maryknoll, N.Y.: Orbis Books, 1983.

Lonergan, B. *Insight.* London: Darton, Longman, and Todd, 1957.

Lonergan, B. *Method in Theology.* Minneapolis: Seabury, 1972.

Mezirow, J. *Transformative Dimensions of Adult Learning.* San Francisco: Jossey-Bass, 1991.

Nouwen, H.J.M. *Reaching Out: The Three Movements of the Spiritual Life.* New York: Doubleday, 1975.

Ó Murchú, D. *Reclaiming Spirituality: A New Spiritual Framework for Today's World.* New York: Crossroad, 1998.

Osborne, K. B. *Lay Ministry in the Roman Catholic Church: Its History and Theology.* Mahwah, N.J.: Paulist Press, 1993.

Palmer, P. J. *To Know as We Are Known: A Spirituality of Education.* San Francisco: Harper San Francisco, 1983.

Rohfeld, R. W., and Zachary, L. J. "Participation in Adult Jewish Learning: Some Implications for Strengthening Jewish Identity and Continuity." *Journal of Jewish Communal Service,* Winter/Spring 1995, pp. 234–241.

Van Ness, P. H. (ed.). *Spirituality and the Secular Quest.* Vol. 22: *World Spirituality: An Encyclopedic History of the Religious Quest.* New York: Crossroad, 1996.

Zachary, L. J., and Burstyn, J. N. "Adult Jewish Learning: Then and Now." *Jewish Education,* 1993, *60* (2), 10–13.

Zachary, L. J. "Adult Jewish Learning: Reshaping the Future." *Agenda: Jewish Education,* 1992, *1* (1), 35–38.

CATHERINE P. ZEPH is assistant professor of religious education and faculty coordinator of LIMEX Instructional Design at the Loyola Institute for Ministry, Loyola University New Orleans.

9

This chapter highlights the challenges of implementing spirituality in adult education practice and offers suggestions for further reading.

Controversy, Questions, and Suggestions for Further Reading

Marie A. Gillen, Leona M. English

In this chapter, we present issues and challenges relating to the spiritual dimensions of adult education. We point out some of the forces that make it difficult to integrate a spiritual dimension into adult education programs, such as lack of understanding about the true meaning of spirituality, lack of practice-related knowledge, and organizational and institutional forces that either block such initiatives or co-opt them to serve their own selfish ends. Finally, we conclude with suggestions for further reading on the topic.

Chapter Themes

In 1925, Basil Yeaxlee wrote about the need for spiritual values in adult education. As the world enters into the new century and the new millennium, the title of this issue reiterates Yeaxlee's summons. Although he claimed that there was a distinction between spirituality and religion, he believed that religion was the ultimate good. In this volume, we make no such claim. In our view, the spiritual dimension of adult education is often broader and more central to human experience than religion. Our vision of spirituality is echoed especially in Jane Vella's opening chapter, in which she refers to the spiritual as "reverence for the other," and in the second chapter, by Linda Vogel, who discusses "connecting the sacred and the ordinary."

Similarly, the third chapter, by Leona English, identifies how the commonplace activities of mentoring, self-directed learning, and dialogue in settings such as health promotion, higher education, and community development contribute to the spiritual development of the adult learner. In all cases, English proposes transforming how one perceives experience so that

NEW DIRECTIONS FOR ADULT AND CONTINUING EDUCATION, no. 85, Spring 2000 © Jossey-Bass Publishers

it becomes more than unreflected, meaningless knowledge. Likewise, in Chapter Four R.E.Y. Wickett examines how the learning covenant can be used to incorporate the spiritual dimension into the learning experience. He identifies seven factors that characterize the learning covenant, including responsibility and commitment. Wickett points out how the learning covenant can increase the learner's self-directness and responsibility on the one hand, and result in a spiritual experience for both educator and learner on the other hand.

In Chapter Five, Lynda W. Miller examines how continuing professional education, especially in the nursing profession, can be imbued with respect and reverence for learning and for all participants. Similarly, in Chapter Six, Jeffrey Orr uses the four directions of the medicine wheel to show how Native ways of knowing and educating, including storytelling and talking circles, can inform adult education practice for both Natives and non-Natives. In Chapter Seven, Wilf Bean uses examples from community development, both national and international, to develop principles that help foster spirituality in adult education and community development and make it relevant. In Chapter Eight, Catherine Zeph draws on her involvement with professional education programs for lay ministry to show how such programs can promote the spirituality of participants.

We hope that this volume disturbs some people's thinking about the spiritual hunger in our time, to the point where they ask themselves this question: How should adult educators respond to this need? To stimulate this discussion, we address some of the questions that spirituality raises, and we challenge our readers to identify their own questions, to respond to our queries, and to engage actively with this text. By bringing this topic more fully into the public arena, we hope to continue a conversation on the spiritual dimensions of adult education that adult education writers such as Weibust and Thomas (1993), Westrup (1998), and Zinn (1997) have already begun.

Issues and Challenges

The first issue raised in this volume is the lack of consensus on the definition of *spirituality*. In their chapters, Bean, Vogel, and Wickett all speak directly to this lack of consensus. They point out that it is difficult to develop a definition that is agreeable to everyone, yet each of the writers in this volume actually tries to define the term. For us, spirituality ranges from an internal experience to an outward sense of commitment to others and the natural order. Although we offer a definition in the Editors' Notes, we imagine that adult educators will react the same as the chapter authors did, making a case for their own definition that is relevant in their particular context. For example, the context of Orr's chapter, which is Native adult education, differs substantially from Miller's context, which is continuing professional education for nurses. In adult education there is a range of contexts, so addressing the spiritual dimensions of learning in the face of such variety becomes a challenging and often daunting task.

The second issue raised in this volume is how adult educators can balance the needs of those who adhere to religious beliefs with those who separate their spirituality from traditional religious institutions. Some chapter authors noted problems resulting from linking spirituality and religion. In this regard, Vogel is very insightful. In Chapter Two she notes that many learners and educators have had negative contacts with religious groups and consequently resist the language of spirituality. She cautions adult educators to be ready for these situations and to have contingencies in place. Zinn (1997) suggests setting ground rules at the outset of discussion that discourage proselytizing and promote respect and a spirit of genuine inquiry in the learning context. Similar rules usually work when debatable topics such as politics, economics, and gun control are raised.

Viewing spirituality and religion as separate entities is challenging for even the most critical of writers and thinkers. The title of a recent thematic issue of the Oxfam journal, *Gender and Development* (1999), promised a thoroughgoing discussion of gender, religion, and spirituality. The editor delivered a disappointing compilation of articles on women, development, and women's involvement in some of the world's religions, without engaging in dialogue on spirituality. The writers in this volume had to struggle with the tension between spirituality and religion, and in all cases they had to find a balance between their own overt religious commitments and the writing of their chapter. Zeph and Miller, for instance, identified their own religious context and commitments; they wrote from particular vantage points that limit the generalizability of their ideas. We recognize that this tension between spirituality and religion is real, and we speculate that this was the reason that Yeaxlee's book, written seventy-five years ago with a decidedly religious outlook, did not have enduring value (Cross-Durant, 1984). Adult educators often find that they have to struggle with this tension in their own educational contexts.

The third issue raised in this volume is whether spirituality can be facilitated. Bean, for instance, gives examples of how his community development scenarios can be applied to spirituality in other settings. Most of the writers believe that spirituality can be fostered to some extent. Admittedly, in some contexts, such as the nurses described in Miller's chapter and the lay ministry candidates described in Zeph's chapter, the context and population make purposeful integration of a spiritual dimension easy to translate. Zinn (1997) argues that adult educators as a group have understood well the "Body-Mind-Spirit" (p. 30) connections; consequently, as a professional group we are well able to take seriously our commitment to teaching the whole person, including their spiritual dimension. Similarly, Apps (1996) has noted the importance of whole-person learning and of "teaching from the heart" (p. 16).

The fourth issue addressed in this volume is whether it is ethical to incorporate spirituality into adult education practice given the highly personalized nature of spiritual development. We are cognizant of Fenwick and Lange's (1998) insightful critique of human resource development (HRD), specifically its co-optation of spiritual matters. Having given this matter some thought, we have come down squarely in favor of addressing the spiritual dimensions in all aspects of adult education practice. Because spirituality is a core part of who we are and "a natural birthright" (Ó Murchú, 1998, p. ix), to neglect the spiritual is equivalent to neglecting the cognitive or emotional dimensions of the learning process.

A graver ethical question is whether adult educators should ignore the spiritual dimension in their practice. Given the general consensus that humans are spiritual beings who seek to make meaning out of life and their experiences, it is imperative that adult educators engage the spiritual and assist learners in making meaning and in answering their deepest questions.

The fifth issue raised here is how adult educators can prepare adequately to embrace the spiritual dimension of their teaching. The task may be daunting and somewhat nebulous; consequently, adult educators may find themselves resisting the task of facilitating, as Vella says in Chapter One, "the spiritual life of self and others." Vogel, in Chapter Two, answers this challenge in part when she challenges educators to reckon with their own spiritual lives, examine critically their own experiences, face critical issues, and nurture their own spiritual lives by engaging in storytelling and by creating and maintaining rituals.

Wise counsel for adult educators, with respect to spirituality, is to take seriously what they already do in adult education practice. For a very long time, professionals in our field have taken seriously the importance of teaching the whole person, including all aspects of their being. In some respects, then, responding to learners' spiritual needs does not demand any additional preparation or require any supernatural gift or teaching ability. Basically, spirituality requires adult educators to challenge themselves continuously, to engage in a critically reflective practice that encourages the questioning of assumptions and beliefs, and to listen carefully to the needs of the learners. This is a spirited epistemology that engages learners in genuine dialogue, builds a commitment to the common good, and establishes "a new commons" (Daloz, Keen, Keen, and Parks, 1996, p. 2) in which to work out community issues and create a new vision for adult education.

Future Directions

Given the trends in spirituality in popular culture, we feel confident that the move to integrate the spiritual dimensions of adult education will continue. As interest grows in uncovering the spiritual dimensions of all of life, from the environment to health care to HRD to movies and popular culture, so shall a similar interest in adult education grow. The recently inaugurated World Commission on Spirituality (Cousins, 1999) is proof that interest is growing and that increased attention will be focused on spirituality in the third millennium. As an indication of the seriousness of this undertaking, commissioners include Nobel Prize winner Elie Wiesel and Bishop Desmond Tutu (Shafer, 1999).

The courageous voice of adult educator Cheryl Hunt (1998) bears stating here. She urges adult educators who subscribe to a reflective practice model to address more openly in their practice spiritual such questions as "Who am I?" Hunt urges practitioners to be closer to their own self-examination, to look to their own selves, and to avoid divorcing themselves from such a vital aspect of self. She refers to this dimension of adult education as spiritual. Hunt's orientation to reflective practice is concerned with how adult educators can integrate their personal selves with their work and ultimately contribute to being effective educators.

At the beginning of the new millennium, adult educators must move forward, drawn by the unknown and buttressed by knowledge from the past. The purpose of this volume is to bring to light the topic of spirituality and in some small way address the paucity of literature on this subject. We have initiated a discussion while at the same time admitting that there is no ready-made way to integrate a spiritual dimension into professional practice. In the words and the spirit of Eduard Lindeman (1982), a seminal adult education figure, we encourage adult educators to become "searchers after wisdom and not oracles" (p. 121); in other words, adult educators need to look for insights in their own experience and in themselves, and ultimately to become creators of their own meaning.

Recommended Reading

The authors of the chapters in this volume have introduced a number of interesting books and articles. We highlight some of these here and suggest others because we believe they will be useful to other researchers and practitioners.

Apps, J. W. *Teaching from the Heart*. Malabar, Fla.: Krieger, 1996.
This book is written for teachers and learners who are interested in learning and teaching from the heart. Apps addresses the issue of whole-person learning, which includes specific attention to the spiritual dimensions of learners. Through telling stories and suggesting specific activities and exercises for learners to use, Apps provides a clear, readable, and usable framework for changing how one teaches and learns. The book also includes a selected bibliography for further reading.

Daloz, L.A.P., Keen, C. H., Keen, J. P., and Parks, S. D. *Common Fire: Leading Lives of Commitment in a Complex World*. Boston: Beacon Press, 1996.
This book reports on a national American study of one hundred adults who were identified as contributing to the common good and who sustained their commitments over an extended period. The writers provide thick, rich

detail from their interviews with the study participants, shedding light on their common concerns, values, commitments, and backgrounds. What emerges is a complex portrait of those who are known to have moral and ethical courage in the course of their everyday life and work. Interestingly, 82 percent of the study's participants classify themselves as having religious or spiritual influences in their lives that have affected their life choices and their commitment to the common good or a quest for meaning.

MacKeracher, D. M. *Making Sense of Adult Learning.* Toronto: Culture Concepts, 1996.

This book provides a spirituality-positive view of adult learning. MacKeracher develops principles of adult learning and offers suggestions for facilitating adult education experiences. Most importantly, she identifies and explores the spiritual dimension of learning and argues convincingly that the spiritual dimension of the learner needs to be engaged, stimulated, and integrated into the adult education experience.

Palmer, P. *The Courage to Teach: Exploring the Inner Landscapes of a Teacher's Life.* San Francisco: Jossey-Bass, 1998.

Palmer's book will help adult educators who are struggling to articulate a personal philosophy of teaching that goes beyond methods, disciplines, and regimentation. Palmer's book is an extended essay on the privilege of teaching, which includes the possibility for meaningful dialogue between teacher and student. He articulates a philosophy of teaching that embraces the spiritual, that challenges teachers to look inside at their "inner landscapes," and that brings their insights to the teaching encounter. This is a soul-filled book that will challenge and inspire educators.

Van Ness, P. H. (ed.). *World Spirituality: An Encyclopedic History of the Religious Quest.* Vol. 22: *Spirituality and the Secular Quest.* New York: Crossroad, 1996.

This edited collection provides accessible discussions of spirituality as experienced in a variety of secular forms such as holistic health, twelve-step programs, and feminism. Van Ness's compilation includes an insightful and critical look at the exponential growth of secular spirituality and its meaning. He points out that an increasing number of Americans find spirituality apart from religious groups, and this phenomenon needs a response.

Zeldin, M., and Lee, S. S. (eds.). *Touching the Future: Mentoring and the Jewish Professional.* Los Angeles: Hebrew Union College—Jewish Institute of Religion, 1995.

This short collection of articles addresses the spirituality of teaching and learning encounters, especially as it is experienced through mentorship. The various authors address mentoring as a discursive, mutual, and reciprocal process. Mentorship case studies point out how mentoring is lived and enacted, and how it provides enlightenment for the educator, the learner, and the learning environment.

References

Apps, J. W. *Teaching from the Heart*. Malabar, Fla.: Krieger, 1996.

Cousins, E. "Spirituality on the Eve of a New Millennium: An Overview." *Chicago Studies*, 1999, *38* (1), 5–14.

Cross-Durant, A. "Basil Yeaxlee and Lifelong Education." *International Journal of Lifelong Education*, 1984, *3* (4), 279–291.

Daloz, L.A.P., Keen, C. H., Keen, J. P, and Parks, S. D. *Common Fire: Leading Lives of Commitment in a Complex World*. Boston: Beacon Press, 1996.

Fenwick, T. J., and Lange, E. "Spirituality in the Workplace: The New Frontier of HRD." *Canadian Journal for the Study of Adult Education*, 1998, *12* (1), 63–87.

Gender and Development, 1999, *7* (1).

Hunt, C. "An Adventure: From Reflective Practice to Spirituality." *Teaching in Higher Education*, 1998, *3* (3), 325–337.

Lindeman, E. C. "To Put Meaning into the Whole of Life." In R. Gross (ed.), *Invitation to Lifelong Learning*. River Grove, Ill.: Follett, 1982.

Ó Murchú, D. *Reclaiming Spirituality*. New York: Crossroad, 1998.

Shafer, I. H. "World Commission on Global Consciousness and Spirituality." [http://globalspirit.org/home.htm]. June 29, 1999.

Weibust, P. S., and Thomas, L. E. "Learning and Spirituality in Adulthood." In J. D. Sinnott (ed.), *Interdisciplinary Handbook of Adult Lifespan Learning*. Westport, Conn.: Greenwood Press, 1993.

Westrup, J. "Invisibility? Spiritual Values and Adult Education." *Australian Journal of Adult and Community Education*, 1998, *38* (2), 106–110.

Yeaxlee, B. A. *Spiritual Values in Adult Education*. 2 vols. London: Oxford University Press, 1925.

Zinn, L. M. "Spirituality in Adult Education." *Adult Learning*, 1997, *8* (5, 6), 26–30.

MARIE A. GILLEN is professor of adult education at St. Francis Xavier University, Antigonish, Nova Scotia, Canada.

LEONA M. ENGLISH is assistant professor of adult education at St. Francis Xavier University, Antigonish, Nova Scotia, Canada.

INDEX

Accountability: in spirited epistemology, 13–14; of teacher to learner, 13–14
Achievement-based objectives, 14
Adult education: challenges of spiritual dimension in, 4–5, 86–88; community development and, 4, 67–75; content in, 23–24; ecological base in, 63–64, 72–73; medicine wheel applied to, 61–65; Native, 59–65; overview of spiritual dimension in, 1–5, 85–86; professionalization of, 67–68; spirited epistemology approach to, 3, 7–15
Adult education master's program, self-directed learning in, 33–34, 41
Adult educators: accountability of, to learners, 13–14; benefits of learning covenants to, 44; demands on, 15; integrity in, 18–19; reflective practice of, 24, 25–26, 89; role of, as midwives, 24; role of, as resource and guide, 11, 24; spiritual lives of, 3, 17–26, 54, 88, 90; support and preparation for, 15, 88; wholeness in, 17–26. *See also* Learning covenants; Teacher-learner relationship
Adult learners: benefits of learning covenants to, 44; in lay ministry programs, 80–81; as Subjects, 7–15, 17, 23, 35, 44, 73–74; teachers' accountability to, 13–14; as whole persons, 17. *See also* Learning covenants; Subject-learner; Teacher-learner relationship
Adult learning: assumptions about, 8–11; principles of, 10, 12, 13; readings about, 90. *See also* Learning
Adult religious education. *See* Lay ministry
Affective dimension of learning, 12, 29
Affirmation, 42
African Xhosa proverb, 74
Ahenakew, F., 64, 65
Ah-Hah, 73
Alexander, A., 69, 75
Andragogy, 61, 62
Annie E. Casey Foundation Jobs Initiative, 8
Antigonish Movement: as example of community development-adult educa-

tion, 68–69, 70, 73; as example of mentoring, 31–32, 36, 69
Apps, J. W., 87, 89, 91
Architectural studio, 24
Ariyaratne, A. T., 70, 71, 75
Assembly-line education, 15
Augustine, St., 7

Bakhtin, M. M., 14, 15, 16
Banking system of education, 9
Barndt, D., 73, 75
Battiste, M., 59, 64, 65
Bean, W. E., 4, 31, 67, 76, 86, 87
Belenky, M. F., 24, 26
Beliefs: origins of, 23; questioning of, 22–23, 25–26. *See also* Critical reflection
Bender, S., 20, 21, 26
Berardinelli, P., 14, 16
Bernier, P., 78, 84
Berry, T., 1–2, 5, 72, 75
Body-mind-spirit connection, 50, 87. *See also Holistic headings*
Bondi, R. C., 19, 26
Brookfield, S. D., 19, 24, 27, 32, 37
Brown-bag lunches, 37
Bruchac, J., 64, 65
Brussat, F., 20, 27, 77, 84
Brussat, M. A., 21, 27, 77, 84
Buddhism, 26; principles of, in Sarvodaya Shramadana community development, 70–71
Burrow, J., 9, 14, 16
Burstyn, J. N., 78, 84

Caduto, M. J., 64, 65
Caffarella, R. S., 32, 37, 46, 47, 56, 57
Calliou, S., 60, 61, 62, 65
Candy, P., 32, 37
Caring for others: as component of nursing education, 50; as component of spiritual development, 30; dialogue and, 35; mentoring and, 32; self-directed learning and, 33
Carter, S. L., 18, 27
Case study method, 25
Cervero, R. M., 49, 57
Challenge, 20, 22, 25

93

Back Issue/Subscription Order Form

Copy or detach and send to:
Jossey-Bass Inc., Publishers, 350 Sansome Street, San Francisco CA 94104-1342

Call or fax toll free!
Phone 888-378-2537 6AM-5PM PST; Fax 800-605-2665

Back issues: Please send me the following issues at $23 each.
(Important: please include series initials and issue number, such as ACE78.)

1. ACE _____

_____

_____

$ _____ Total for single issues

$ _____ Shipping charges (for single issues *only;* subscriptions are exempt
from shipping charges): Up to $30, add $5^{50} • $30^{01}–$50, add $6^{50}
$50^{01}–$75, add $7^{50} • $75^{01}–$100, add $9 • $100^{01}–$150, add $10
Over $150, call for shipping charge.

Subscriptions   Please ❑ start   ❑ renew my subscription to *New Directions
for Adult and Continuing Education* for the year _____ at the
following rate:

    ❑ Individual $58   ❑ Institutional $104
NOTE: Subscriptions are quarterly, and are for the calendar year only.
Subscriptions begin with the spring issue of the year indicated above.
For shipping outside the U.S., please add $25.

$ _____ Total single issues and subscriptions (CA, IN, NJ, NY and DC
residents, add sales tax for single issues. NY and DC residents must
include shipping charges when calculating sales tax. NY and Canadian
residents only, add sales tax for subscriptions.)

❑ Payment enclosed (U.S. check or money order only)

❑ VISA, MC, AmEx, Discover Card #_____ Exp. date_____

Signature _____ Day phone _____

❑ Bill me (U.S. institutional orders only. Purchase order required.)

Purchase order #_____

Name _____

Address _____

_____

_____

Phone_____ E-mail _____

For more information about Jossey-Bass Publishers, visit our Web site at:
www.josseybass.com   **PRIORITY CODE = ND1**